STINKIN' SPOUSE STINKIN' HEART

By

Dr. Rich Murphy

Maranatha Life
1001 Paradise Cir.

"Stinkin' Spouse - Stinkin' Heart"

Unless otherwise noted, all scriptures taken from the Holy Bible, King James Version.

Published by:
Maranatha Life
1001 Paradise Cir.
Palmview, TX 78572

e-mail: RAMMaraLif@yahoo.com
http://www.MaranathaLife.com

Dedication

I dedicate this book

To God the Father, who made me,

God the Son, who saved me,

And God the Holy Spirit, who is ever changing me.

Acknowledgements

I'd like to thank my wife for putting up with me, all the years that the Holy Spirit has been working on me, and teaching me the things that I've written about in this book. She deserves a medal.

I'd also like to thank my good friend, Pastor Mike Govan, without who I seriously doubt that I would have written this book. His friendship has helped to restore me to the word that God has called me to, and the devil has tried to steal from me.

Finally, I'd like to thank Eli Flores, who designed the cover art for me. Eli is a great guy and a great artist. He was able to take my ideas and turn them into something really special.

TABLE OF CONTENTS

Forward

1.Intro – Everybody's problem 6

2.A marriage made in heaven? 17

3.Those pesky little irritations 24

4.What's wrong with my spouse? 33

5.Voices in your head 41

6.What's in your heart? 49

7.What's God doing to me? 57

8.Your rights and responsibilities in marriage 63

9.Yeah, but they... 71

10.It doesn't matter what they do 79

11.The power of a forgiving heart 87

12.Recognizing your own faults 97

13.What do you expect? 105

14.Quitting the blame game 112

15.Getting rid of false assumptions 120

16.Focusing on the good 126

17.Learning to love unconditionally 135

18.Let not the sun go down... 143

19.So where do you go from here? 149

Stinkin' Spouse Stinkin' Heart

What if God designed marriage to make us holy,

more than to make us happy?

Gary Thomas, Sacred Marriage

Forward

Warning: This is not your typical marriage book.

In fact, some would wonder if this qualifies as a marriage book at all. It's not filled with cute little stories about couples who had problems, nor how they overcame those problems. Nor it is filled with the wisdom that comes from years of learning how to live with someone else. You're not going to find a bunch of great ideas on how to be more romantic, improve your communications or have a better sex life either.

However, if you apply the principles that you'll discover in this book, I can guarantee you, it will transform your marriage. Not because you have learned the secrets of great relationships, but because you've learned the secrets of being a great person to be in a relationship with. It will change the way you approach your marriage and your spouse; and ultimately, that will change your marriage for the better.

Let me tell you a little about where this book came from.

About ten years ago I had an entire year of emotional crisis. We had been missionaries, working along the Texas/Mexico border and living in an old Winnebago motorhome. That was hard on my family, especially after nine years. Our kids had grown and two were in college by then. It was truly time for something better. But we didn't make much money as missionaries and we couldn't afford anything more.

Then my wife came to me one day and asked my agreement on her going back to work as a teacher, so that we could get out of the motorhome and into a house. I wasn't really in agreement, but I said okay anyway. The original plan was for her to work part-time, as a substitute, so that she could continue working with me in the ministry. That plan lasted for about a half a day.

The first school district my wife applied at sent her to one of their middle schools, where they hired her on the spot as a "permanent substitute," something that supposedly doesn't exist. So she was working full-time and didn't have any time for the ministry. Not only that, but she really didn't have any time for the family or for me either. Teachers work hard, at least conscientious ones do, and they deserve their summers off even more than the kids do.

My wife was an excellent teacher, but it was her dedication to her job that ended up making an emotional mess of me. Don't take me wrong; that wasn't her fault. But her job and the demands it put upon her were the trigger.

The next year was the worst one of my life. But it was one in which I learned some very valuable lessons; many of which are included in this book. God proved Himself faithful, meeting me in my darkest hours and using those to mold and shape me more and more into the image of His Son; my Lord, Jesus Christ.

I was taken back to a key verse in Isaiah, which God had shown me many years ago.

> *When the (spiritually and emotionally) poor and needy seek water, and there is none, and their tongue faileth for thirst, I the Lord will hear them, I the God of Israel will not forsake them. 18 I will open rivers in high places, and fountains in the midst of the*

valleys: I will make the wilderness a pool of water, and the dry land springs of water. [19] I will plant in the wilderness the cedar, the shittah tree, and the myrtle, and the oil tree; I will set in the desert the fir tree, and the pine, and the box tree together: [20] That they may see, and know, and consider, and understand together, that the hand of the Lord hath done this, and the Holy One of Israel hath created it.

Isaiah 41:17-20 parenthesis mine

Those verses were given to me at a time when I was going through a wilderness experience. I won't take the time here to go into detail about them, but they talk of the work that the Holy Spirit does in us during those times. Water symbolizes the Word of God in prophecy and trees represent growth and strength. There are four types of waters mentioned, showing us four different ways that the Lord plants his Word in us. There are also seven different types of trees, each of which refers to a different type of growth that happens in us. I was in the wilderness and God was working on me there.

As He has done many times previously, God gave me a new verse in this wilderness time:

For whom he did foreknow, he also predestined to be conformed to the image of His Son, that he might be firstborn among many brethren.

Romans 8:29

Once we are saved, this is God's biggest goal in our lives... to remake us into the image of Jesus. This has become the center of my life and my ministry for the last 10 years, learning how to apply this concept to my life and helping others learn it too. This is the central theme of this book.

If we want our marriages to change, then we need to quit trying to get God to change our spouse and start allowing Him to change us. We can't change them, but we can change ourselves. Through that, we can transform our marriages.

This book is a journey. It's about transformation. Wherever you are today is the starting point. Through these chapters, I hope to take you from there, to a better you and through that to a better marriage. That's not something that can happen in a few hours of reading, but rather, in the hours that you spend thinking about what you've read and allowing God to mold tem into your heart and life.

Please don't take the things you read in these pages and try to throw them onto your spouse. If all you see here is where they are failing, I haven't done my job. You need to see yourself in these concepts and how you are falling short of becoming all that you can to be a perfect spouse. That's where the benefit comes from.

Don't try to read this book through, from cover to cover. It's not that type of book. If that's all you do, you won't get much out of it. Rather, read it a chapter at a time. They're short, but powerful. Then allow what you've learned in each chapter to work in your heart. Go back and reread a chapter, if you need to. Take your time on this journey and allow the Holy Spirit to do His work.

More than anything, ask the Holy Spirit to use what you read in this book to work on your heart. Ask Him to show you the truth about yourself; what you are truly like. We all struggle to see ourselves clearly, but when we ask, the Holy Spirit will show us.

I pray that the things that you learn in this book will be beneficial to you; helping you to be more like Christ and to demonstrate Christ-likeness to your spouse. I don't want you to have to go through the ten years that it cost me to learn these concepts, or even worse, never learn them. It would be better if you could have a shorter journey. If this book has a part in doing that a little bit, I have accomplished what I have set out to do.

May God richly bless you and your spouse, as you begin this journey.

1

Everybody's Problem

Let's start out with the basics. For us, that means starting with the marriage relationship. When we look at marriages today, we find that there are a lot of misconceptions, a lot of bad advice and more than anything, a lot of marriage problems. Pretty much everyone has problems in their marriage.

Oh, there are the occasional couples who have either managed to work out a way to peacefully coexist, truly have managed to stay in love, or are just good at faking one of these two options. But basically, everyone has problems. Take a survey of any church congregation and you'll find that all those marriages that you thought were so wonderful, really aren't as wonderful as you thought.

But could that data be skewed? Could it be that our marriages are actually much better than we give them credit for? Could it even be possible that all the conflict we have in our marriages serves a useful purpose? Has God made us with the idea of us constantly being at each other's throats or could he have something better in mind?

To start with, we have to get rid of the fairytale fantasy idea of marriage. Yes, marriage is good, in fact even great, but it isn't perfect. That's not because God didn't create it perfectly, but rather that it is carried out by imperfect people. As long as we, the married people, are imperfect, our marriages will be imperfect too.

But that's okay. In fact, it's something that we should accept and give God thanks for. As long as we are focused on complaining about our marriages and our spouses, we will not garner the full benefit of the marriage that God has given us.

So what is that full benefit? It is to work together to be remade into the image of Jesus Christ, our Lord and Savior. Everything else is secondary to that. Yes, we should love each other and yes we should enjoy being married to each other. But if that's all we get out of marriage, we're missing the point. More importantly, we're missing God's point.

God knew when He created us that we were an imperfect, flawed creation. He could have created us perfect. But had He done that, He would have had nothing more than a bunch of robots. He might have loved them, but there is no way that they could have loved Him back. To give us the ability to love, He had to give us free will and that's where our imperfections come in. The sad truth is that most of us use our free will to be selfish and self-centered, rather than to love those around us.

You can see what I'm talking about by looking at any baby. By their very nature, babies are the most self-centered creatures on the face of the earth. As far as they are concerned, from their limited perspective on life, they are the center of the universe. The whole world exists to serve them. All they have to do is cry and everyone jumps to fulfill their latest desire.

Parents have to work hard to remove this self-centeredness from their children and replace it with something better. Some never succeed. As we look around ourselves at other people we know, we see plenty of examples of self-centeredness in those who are supposed to be mature; we might even see it in our own marriage.

Self-centeredness is the opposite of what love is. It is definitely not one of the fruit of the Spirit. In fact, it is something that we, as Christians, must work to overcome in our lives. If we are ever going to become the people who God has created us to be, self-centeredness is one of the first things that has got to go.

I say that because self-centeredness gets in the way of pretty much all of the other changes we have to make. You see, we are a work in process. God's goal in our life, after salvation, is to remake us into the perfect image of His Son, Jesus, who is called the Christ.

> *For whom he did foreknow, he also predestined to be conformed to the image of His Son, that he might be firstborn among many brethren.*
>
> *Romans 8:29*

You're going to see this verse a lot in this book. That's because it is central to what I want to talk to you about. This one verse has been the focus of my life for over a decade. The Holy Spirit's work in our lives is a transforming one, focused on helping us to conform to the image of Christ.

God has given us an excellent means of seeing our own self-centeredness. It is hidden in the marriage relationship. Specifically, when we see the flaws in our own spouse, they are a means of seeing the failings in our own hearts. That's not to say that those faults aren't real; but rather, that our reaction to them is what shows us where we fall short of the glory of God.

We, all of us, men and women alike, have to stop looking at our spouses as a recipient for our blame and start using them as a tool to show us what is in our own heart. We have to stop focusing on the bad that they do, or that we perceive that they do, and start focusing on the faulty reaction we have to it. We have to start recognizing our own faults, rather than focusing on theirs.

Let me ask you something; if you go to God and complain about your spouse, how will He respond to you? Those who have had that experience know that God isn't going to agree with them, but rather talk to them about their own problems. While God will accept our prayers about helping our spouses, He will never accept our "prayers" which are actually nothing more than thinly veiled complaints.

Yes, God is interested in our spouse's problems. But that is between them and God, not between us and God. So God isn't going to listen to us complain and He certainly isn't going to listen to us give Him instruction on how He should be dealing with them.

Rather, He is going to turn the tables on us and deal with us about ourselves. He is going to take the opportunity that we handed Him, and use it to take care of some area where we are failing.

Let's take a common situation that many marriages encounter, a true stereotype of the marriage relationship. A wife is driving the car and ends up in a minor fender-bender. She is able to drive the car home, but there is no way she can hide the damage to it. When her husband arrives, he sees the damaged car and walks into the house with smoke coming out of his ears, ready to lay into her for "destroying" their car.

Okay, let's freeze frame that scene for a moment. To start with, I'm sure that the wife is already uncomfortable about the situation and afraid of her husband's reaction. There's a good chance she's been crying. He has probably blown up at her before and she knows what to expect. There's even a fairly good chance that she believes that she deserves it, especially if she was at fault.

Now let's look at the husband. The first question that comes to my mind is whether he loves his wife more or the car more. If he truly loved his wife, wouldn't he be more concerned about her, than he is about the car? Shouldn't he be running in the door to make sure that she's okay, rather than in a fit of rage? On top of that question, I have to ask myself how materialistic the man is. If he were heavenly focused, rather than earthly focused, would the damaged car bother him that much?

Yes, damage to the car is expensive and dealing with the problems it causes costs way more than just what the body shop charges. But when push comes to shove, it's just a car. It's an inanimate object; a tool. Something we buy to make our life easier; nothing more.

If that man were to go to God, seeking for God to change his wife's "careless ways," God would probably ignore his request. Oh, she might be careless, but you'd never know it from the way that God would respond to the man. God would turn the tables on him and start talking about his lack of love towards his wife, his anger problem and his overabundance of love for material things. He'd probably even throw in something about his lack of focus on the eternal, just for good measure.

What is important to us isn't necessarily important to God. In fact, it probably isn't important to God. We can find what is important to God in the Bible, and that is clearly souls. He cares about people and the condition of their hearts. Everything else is secondary.

Situations like this, where we show what is truly in our hearts, are played out over and over again, each and every day of our lives. Yet we usually miss the lessons that they can teach us.

We spend so much time focused on the failings of others, specifically the failings of our spouses, that we fail to see the important things that God wants to show us about our own hearts.

If you want a truly great marriage, than you must do everything you can to make the people in it better. Since you can't change your spouse, that means you need to concentrate on changing yourself.

So why don't we do this? There are several reasons. First of all, our emotions get in the way. All too often, we allow ourselves to be ruled by our emotions, rather than taking dominion over them. But emotions are fickle; they are dangerous. They show us things that aren't true as if they are. Since we live in a negative world and we have learned negativity from it, our emotions often take things that should be good and turn them to bad.

One of the biggest areas of emotional baggage that confronts us in marriage is that of disappointment. When we are dating, we see that other person, who eventually becomes our spouse, as perfect. That's not because they are, it's because we are in love, which causes us to perceive them to be perfect. Hence, the common saying that "love is blind."

But eventually the blinders come off of our eyes, and we start seeing that person for who they are. As time goes on, we see more and more of the negative, focusing on it, and less and less of the positive. This causes pretty much everyone to feel as if they have been "tricked into marriage." They feel that the person that they dated has changed, or that they were putting on an act all along.

Let me answer that. Yes, they were putting on an act. Dating isn't real life; it's phony. It's all about presenting your best side to the other person. But that's much easier to do when you aren't with them all the time. Once you are married, you lose the ability to hide from them and allow the real you to come out. Your spouse ends up seeing the real you and you end up seeing the real them.

But there's something that makes this even worse; that's pre-marital intimacy, especially sexual intercourse. That's why God tells us to remain sexually pure until marriage. Sex before marriage destroys our ability to see the other person as they really are. Any physical touch, but especially intimate contact, releases the hormone oxytocin into our bodies, which causes the emotional sensation of feeling "in love." Whenever the physical contact reduces after marriage, and it pretty much always does, there is less oxytocin in our bodies, and we "fall out of love."

The problem then, is that we usually don't any have real love to replace being in love. So our attitude towards our spouse changes drastically, and not for the better. We start to see the faults that were there all along and our attitude towards them begins to change.

Perhaps if God hadn't made us in such a way that we would have the feelings of being in love it would have prevented this problem. But I've got to say that if he had done that, there's a good chance that we never would have gotten married. So we wouldn't have received the benefits of marriage, the help it can be to perfect us and the joy that it can bring.

If we are ever going to receive those benefits to the full, we've got to change the way we are looking at marriage. We've got to stop focusing on the perceived bad in our spouse, and start focusing on the real bad that there is within us. We've got to be willing to change. We've got to allow the Holy Spirit to show us what is inside us that needs to come out, and then we've got to become an active participant in that process.

It's time to get rid of the fairy-tale view of marriage and start seeing it for what it really is, a partnership, forged in heaven, and designed to help both marriage partners reach the fullness of what God has created them to be. Then, and only then, will we reach our full potential.

But the good news is this. Throwing away the fairy-tale marriage fantasy is probably the best way of realizing that sort of marriage. When the two of you allow God to remake you into who you need to be, you will start fulfilling each other and start transforming your marriage. Not so much because of the changes that your spouse makes, but because of the changes that you choose to make.

In case you haven't noticed, life is about change. It is called the only true constant. But not all change is good. One can change for the better or change for the worst. It all depends on the choices that they make. You choose to change in ways that will make you a better, more Christ-like person, or by not making that choice you effectively choose to change in ways that make you more like the negative world that we live in.

This book is about those changes. Everything in here talks about changes that I have had to make in my own life. None of them were easy, but each of them was beneficial. I have found that by changing myself, I am able to be more of a blessing to my wife, doing a better job of fulfilling the commandment in Ephesians 5:25, *"Husbands, love your wives, even as Christ also loved the church, and gave himself for it."*

Action Items:

- Repent before God for throwing past teachings you've heard onto your spouse. Make a commitment to look first at yourself and see where any message you hear might apply to you.
- Commit to stop focusing on the negative you see about your spouse and to start looking for the positive.
- Pray and ask the Holy Spirit to show you the failings in your own heart.

2

A MARRIAGE MADE IN HEAVEN

We've all heard about that one couple who has a perfect marriage, a "marriage made in heaven." At least, that's the way it looks to outsiders. Nobody else sees the strife and abuse that may be going on behind closed doors, and if the couple are good enough at acting, they always appear madly in love when they are in front of others.

None of us really knows what goes on in other people's marriages, unless we live with them. We don't even know what goes on in our closest friend's marriages. Rather, all we know is the public image that they portray and the more secretive information that they tell us. But even our closest friends are only going to tell us one side of the story. It might look very different from their spouse's point of view.

Yet there is a great tendency to compare our marriage to others. Let me just say that that's not a good idea. Whenever we compare our marriage to another, we always come up short. Since we don't see what's really going on in those other people's hearts, we assume things are better than they are, and we are already convinced of how bad they are in our own marriages.

While there might actually be marriages made in heaven, they are not perfect marriages in the sense that we understand the term. In fact, I'll go so far as to say that any marriage that God puts together is going to be one in which the two partners grate on each other constantly.

How can I say that? It's easy. When we think of a marriage made in heaven, we're thinking of happiness. Somehow or other, we've gotten the idea that happiness is the ultimate goal of any marriage. As such, when there isn't enough happiness in the marriage, we seem to think that the marriage couldn't be ordained by God. I'd blame this on Hollywood and how they've portrayed marriage; but then, the idea that marriage is supposed to make us happy existed long before Hollywood did.

Of course, Hollywood really can't teach anything of value about marriage. They are more adept at divorce and affairs than they are at marriage. So if you have taken any marriage advice from them, I'd suggest burning it or at least throwing it out with the garbage.

God is concerned about much bigger things than our happiness; He's concerned with the condition of our soul. Therefore, if we allow God to choose our mate for us, He will pick someone who will help us to grow and mature, not someone who will make us happy. Oh, there will be some happiness along the way, but that will be incidental, not intentional. True happiness in marriage is reached when the couple matures together, becoming molded more and more into the image of Christ.

Few of us actually allow God the chance of choosing our mate. We are emotionally driven to find someone who we can join together with, sharing our lives and reproducing ourselves in our children. As such, we look for someone to fulfill that role, usually without even asking God's opinion.

Of course, I seriously doubt that most of us would accept

God's opinion, even if He offered it. The drive to find a mate and to be "in love" is so strong, that it blinds us to reality. That's actually good in a way, as it prevents us from seeing the other person's flaws. If we see them, we might just run the other way and never get married.

When we compare what men and women look for in a potential spouse with what men and women are created to be and what part they fulfill in marriage, we find a huge disparity:

- **Women** look for a man who is romantic and fulfills her emotional desires. She wants that white knight who will sweep her off her feet. If he's romantic enough in her eyes, she won't even notice if he is able to hold down a job.

- **Men** look for a woman who is beautiful and sexy, almost to the point of totally ignoring her character and personality. If she is sexy enough, he is sure that he'll be happy with her.

In both of these cases, the person we are looking for is nothing like the person we need.

- A **sexy woman** won't necessarily be a good mother, a good helpmeet, or a good homemaker. For that matter, she might not even be good at sex. She might have suffered sexual abuse as a child and the whole idea of sex freaks her out.

- A **romantic man** may not be a good provider. He may not have the first idea of how to be a husband and father. He may not be a good protector. In fact, other than meeting her emotional needs, he may not be capable of meeting any other need that she has.

But even if I'm wrong, and the person you marry can actually fulfill the classic male/female roles, that's not going to make you happy. For you see, what we look for in a dating relationship, when we are supposedly looking for our spouse, has absolutely nothing to do with who they are created to be, or how we will fulfill our responsibilities once we are married.

- **Women** look for a romantic man, and marry him. Then, if he's a good man, he works hard to provide for her. He was created to protect and provide, that's his nature, not to fulfill all her emotional needs. So as he's busy going about the work of doing what he has been created to do, she becomes disillusioned and dissatisfied because he's not as romantic as he was before.

- **Men** look for that sexy woman and marry her. Then, if she is a good woman, she sets about taking care of the home, nurturing her husband and eventually her children. She becomes a strong helpmeet, providing him with an emotional atmosphere of support, so that he can do the best at what he does. That's her nature; how God created her. But she may not fully satisfy him sexually, giving him as much as he wants.

Please note that I am not saying that husbands shouldn't concern themselves with their wives emotional needs; nor am I saying that wives should not concern themselves with their husband's sexual needs. What I'm saying is that who we are created to be isn't what the opposite sex thinks we are. God created us hard wired to do certain things. Those are things that are necessary for the fulfillment of our lives and purpose here on this earth. Not things that are focused on our happiness.

God's part in our marriages is that he is the one approves and sanctifies our marriages. Regardless of whether or not we ask Him to find us a spouse and marry the person He brings to us, he is the one to put his seal of approval on our marriage. In fact, there are really only three options for the believer, and they all end with God's stamp of approval.

- We asked God to bring us the perfect spouse for us and He did. In that case, our marriage has his seal of approval from the very beginning.

- We ignore God's advice and marry who we choose. Since God created marriage, declaring *"it is not good for man to be alone"* (Gen 2:18), He puts His seal of approval on our marriage the day of the wedding.

- We marry before accepting Christ. In that case, we leave God out of our marriage. But the day that we receive Jesus as our Lord and Savior, He puts His seal of approval on our marriage.

In this sense, all of us have a marriage made in heaven. God has approved of it, because we are fulfilling his plan for our lives. He is happy we are married and even happier when we act out our love for one another in godly ways.

But let me define what I mean by God's "seal of approval." First of all, I mean the obvious, that God approves of our marriage relationship. But even more than that, God takes the marriage as it is and begins to use it to mold and shape us into the image of His Son. By marrying, we give God one more tool (actually more than one) which He can use to work on our hearts.

We may not always enjoy that process, especially when our spouse does something that we don't like. But by faith we have to accept that each and every one of those things is for our benefit. After all, *"All things work together for good, to them that love God, to them who are called according to his purpose"* (Rom 8:28). That's not an excuse for what happens in our lives, its God's plan and purpose.

A lot of people have used that verse to try and explain away a lot of bad in people's lives. That's not what I am doing. What I'm saying is that amongst its other purposes, one of the purposes which God has for marriage is to shape and change us through it.

So stop looking at your spouse as a curse in your life and start accepting them for what they are; a blessing from God. Yes, that person who annoys you so much is really a blessing. Even the things they do to annoy you are a blessing. All you need to do is accept the blessing and learn how to use it for your betterment.

What kind of betterment? Improving the person that you are, turning you into a new and improved, better you.

If there is one thing that will show the flaws in our character, it is marriage. Our spouses, who should receive the best we have to offer, often only receive the leftovers. That's because there are so many relationships that we have, where we have to be on our best behavior. We can't act as we would want to act, because it could have negative consequences.

If you don't believe me, just try telling your boss off some day. You may just find that you're in the unemployment line the next. That boss doesn't have to put up with your emotional garbage, there's always someone else to do your job.

But when we are home, we feel that we can let our guard down. The real us comes out of hiding, and I'll have to say, that real us isn't all that pretty. It's selfish and self-centered, wanting its own way all the time, and it throws a temper tantrum if it doesn't get it.

This is the person that God wants to work on. Literally, it's the old man, the carnal man; the one that's supposed to be dead. But he's often quite alive in all of us, because we haven't killed him yet. You see, killing him is a slow, painful process, not something that happens in a moment at the altar. We have to kill him and break his hold in each and every area of our lives, area by area, one at a time.

Each and every irritation from our spouse helps us to identify one more area where the carnal man is still holding on; one more area in which we need to kill the old man. As he dies in those areas, we find real change in our lives and in our hearts, changes that make us more into the image of Christ.

Action Items:

- Make a decision to accept your spouse the way they are, not the way you imagine they are supposed to be. Give thanks to God for the way that they are.
- Throw out the idea that you have a "bad marriage." Thank God that you have a marriage and that He has placed His seal of approval on it.
- Start practicing looking at your spouse with new eyes, ones that see them as a blessing, rather than a curse.

3

THOSE PESKY LITTLE IRRITATIONS

Let me let you in on a little secret here – my wife does things that irritate me. I know that's shocking, but then, I do things that irritate her as well. It's not really intentional on either of our parts... at least most of the time. It's just something that happens. We both have habits that the other finds irritating. It's just a part of what's different about each of us.

Life is full of irritations. If you spend enough time with anyone, you'll find that they have any number of little habits that irritate you. It doesn't matter how good your relationship is or how much you love them, you will find yourself irritated... if you let yourself.

What we usually do with our friends, is to let those irritations go, ignoring them as best we can. But an irritating habit that we allow our friends to have may not seem all that big, simply because we don't spend all that much time with them. On the other hand, we spend a whole lot more time with our spouse, so we are much more likely to find that their irritating habits are getting under our skin, crawling around in there and making us itch all over.

Okay, maybe I'm getting a little carried away there; but you know what I mean. One person might have a habit of humming out of tune and the other is a music connoisseur. I guarantee you, that would be more than just a little irritating. I know, because two of my kids are musicians and I can't carry a tune if you put it in a box and hand the box to me. Maybe that's why I don't sing around them.

Have you ever wondered why those things irritate you? Could it be that you just want life to fit into your own mold and are bothered when it doesn't? Are we really just getting irritated because we can't have everything the way that we want?

All of us have certain "norms" in our lives. These are the ways we expect things to be. Many of those came out of our childhood and were actually learned from our parents. As long as those norms are maintained, everything is fine and we are comfortable. But when something comes along that falls outside of those norms, we are suddenly faced with something that makes us decidedly uncomfortable or inconvenienced and we don't want that.

Just look at the huge things that cause irritation for most people: whether the toilet paper is over or under, which way we squeeze the toothpaste tube, how and where things are put away. None of these are major issues, yet they can irritate us to the point where they seem to be major.

One of the classic irritations in marriage is men throwing their dirty clothes on the floor, instead of putting them in the clothes hamper or basket. Many a woman has wasted days, weeks, even months worth of cumulative time fuming about her sloppy husband and his inability to put his dirty clothes where they belong.

But how long would it take her to pick up his clothes and put them in the hamper? Ten seconds; maybe twenty per day? Yet instead of spending that 20 seconds a day picking up his clothes, she wastes 15 minutes a day fuming about it. Not only that, but she allows that little thing to get in the way of having a close and loving marriage. Those dirty clothes literally become more important than her marriage.

Granted, he should probably put the dirty clothes in the hamper himself. But I'm not dealing with him, I'm dealing with you. I don't care how hard you try; you're probably going to have very little success in changing even one of your spouse's irritating habits, let along changing them all.

I don't care if you're a man or a woman; it's easier to change yourself and your habits, than it is to change your spouse and their habits. So why not concentrate on what you can do, instead of fuming about the things you can't?

My wife has an irritating little habit in our bathroom. She leaves her bottles of rubbing alcohol and other things right on the edge of the sink. I literally can't turn the water on, without knocking one of those bottles over. Serious problem, right?

No, it's not. It was years before I even mentioned it to my wife, and when I did, it was with the attitude of laughing at myself and explaining how I blew it off. I'm strong enough to pick up a bottle and move it six inches; and while I'm busy, I'm not so busy that I really don't have time to do so.

You see, when I first noticed my wife leaving that bottle out of place, I could have gotten irritated about it, but I chose not to. I'm a highly organized person, so my nature is to be bothered by things like that. But God doesn't want me to be bothered by it, except in the sense of letting it show me that I have an area in my life that hasn't grown up yet; an area in my heart that needs to be dealt with.

If I let that bottle bother me, I'm literally being childish. I'm essentially saying, "It has to be my way and nothing else is acceptable." But that bathroom sink is as much hers, as it is mine. So what gives me the right to impose my will on how she does things in the bathroom? That's her stuff. She has a right to do it however she sees fit; and if I don't like that, it's up to me to change. It's not up to me to change her.

Everything that irritates us demonstrates to us an area where we are trying to say, "It has to be my way." But you know something? None of it has to be our way. If anything, it has to be God's way. Unless we can find something in scripture that demonstrates to us that our spouse is doing something against the will of God, we're best off keeping our mouths shut.

So what do we do? We learn to blow it off. We put that irritating thing in perspective and realize how small it really is. That might mean figuring out how long it would take for us to move the item, how much money they are wasting, or how much the irritating action affect our lives. Then compare that to how much time and energy we are wasting in being irritated by it. I'll guarantee you; your irritation will come out on the sort end, every single time.

Now don't go twisting what I'm saying out of shape here. I'm not telling you to allow your spouse to walk all over you, so don't say that I am. Picking up your husband's laundry or putting gas in your wife's car isn't being walked on; it's just putting up with unimportant things. We've all got to learn how to tell the difference between those, and the really important ones. Otherwise, we're going to waste all our ammo fighting wars that don't really matter.

I'm also saying that we need to value our spouses for who they are, more than we need to devalue them for what they don't do the way we want. We all made a commitment "till death do us part." Yet we are allowing other things to try and part us; things that don't really matter. We literally blow their value up; making it seem greater than the person we married.

Yes, there are things that are big enough to be a problem. But the ones I mentioned a moment ago sure don't fall into that category. You probably had a chuckle for each one I said. Why is that? Because you instantly realized how small they really are. Well, so are the irritations that are bothering you.

Let me take this out of the context of marriage for a moment, in order to illustrate how unimportant it is. Most of us have a boss somewhere. I've had several of them though the course of my life. Some were good and then there were others who... well, we won't talk about them.

But even the good ones had their faults. I can't really say that any of them have been perfect. I guess that's just one more part of the fallen nature of man. It shows up at work too.

Even so, each of those bosses filled an important place in my life, at least as long as I was working for them. During that time, I mostly ignored the little things they did which I found irritating. I understood the value of that relationship, so didn't want to allow something insignificant to disturb it.

Yet those people were just my bosses. They really weren't the most important people in my life. Those positions are reserved for my God, my wife, my kids and my closest friends. So if I could ignore those irritating habits my various bosses had, why can't I do so with my spouse?

Could it be that we don't really value our spouse as we should? The day of our wedding, they were the most important, most valuable person in our lives. Did we lose that sense of value along the way? Did we... gulp... start to take them for granted? If we did, whose fault was that?

I know a case of a woman who was married to a very abusive man. She suffered a lot in that marriage and eventually ended up divorcing him. Biblically, she had grounds to do so, since he had committed adultery numerous times.

Eventually, this woman fell in love with another man and married him. As is normal at the beginning of any relationship, she was convinced that he was her White Knight, who had come along to sweep her off on the wings of love. At least... she thought that for a while. But while her new husband was a good man and treated her well, he wasn't perfect. Eventually, she began to become irritated at him, allowing his flaws to become bigger in her eyes, than his worth.

What changed? It wasn't him. It was her perspective. She stopped seeing how good a man he was and started focusing on things that really didn't matter. Those little irritations became big ones, to the point where she talked about her second husband as being as bad as her first. Yet he never abused her, never committed adultery, and loved her every day of their lives.

Quite literally, what should have been a fairy tale ending, became a life of disappointment, irritation and strife. And you know something; it was she who chose to make it that way.

Let me share a secret with you here. You don't have to be irritated. For that matter, you don't have to be mad either. Both irritation and anger are your choice; nobody else's.

If we were talking face to face right now and I threw a bucket of ice cold water on you, how would you react? Some people would become angry at that. They might say to me, "You made me wet and you made me angry." But in reality, all I did was to make you wet. You chose to get angry on your own. You could have just as easily chosen to laugh and maybe get back at me. It was your choice.

Nobody has control over our emotions, except us. We decide what we allow to bother us and what we don't. If we decide that something isn't going to bother us, no matter how much it has in the past, then it can no longer bother us.

It may seem like you don't have any control over your emotions, but trust me, you do. It usually doesn't seem like it, because we are allowing our emotions to control us, rather than us controlling them. That's dangerous. It's about like walking in a mine field, blindfolded. Eventually, you're going to hit a mine.

But you and I have been given control over those emotions. We just need to exercise it, making some wise decisions and not allowing foolishness to be out guide. When we do that, things that previously seemed like huge irritations, will begin to be seen in the light of what they are. We may even find ourselves laughing about the things we used to let bother us.

So what is it going to be? Are you going to laugh off the irritating habits of your spouse or are you going to let them get under your skin. The choice is yours; choose wisely.

Action Items:

- Make a list of the things that irritate you about your spouse and offer them on the altar, before God. Burning the list might be a good way to do this. Then resolve never to allow those things to irritate you again.
- Find something humorous, but not cruel, about the things that irritate you. That will help you to see them in a new light.

- Change the value you place on your spouse, in your mind. Keep elevating it, until they are the single most important thing to you, besides your relationship with God.

- Begin taking control over your emotions and not allowing them to control you. Decide how you are going to feel about something, and base that decision on something solid, like how much that person is worth in your life.

4

WHAT'S WRONG WITH MY SPOUSE?

I don't care who you are, at some point in your life, you're going to end up asking yourself the question, "What's wrong with my spouse?" Women ask it about their husbands and men ask it about their wives. The first time is usually just shortly after the honeymoon is over, and you'll continue asking yourself that question for years; probably for the rest of your life. The only real issue is how often you ask it of yourself.

So, what is wrong with your spouse? Let's start with the premise that there is something wrong with them. In fact, we can say with great confidence that there is something wrong with every person who has ever been born. We all share the same problems, which probably exist because ultimately we share the same parents.

If we go all the way back to Genesis, we find that God created two people, named Adam and Eve. Adam, which literally means "man" was created first and then God put him to sleep to perform the first ever rib transplant, taking one of Adam's ribs and turning it into the first woman, Eve.

I think we can take it for granted that Adam and Eve were the best, most perfect people ever created. They were physically perfect specimens of the human species, with high intellect and unmarred by childhood trauma. They had an opportunity that nobody has had since, that of ruling the world, without having to fight a war to conquer it. God Himself gave them that right as a wedding gift.

Yet Adam and Eve, as perfect as they were, were flawed; they were human. Even though they were made in God's image and His likeness, they weren't gods. Even though they were God's children, they didn't carry his DNA. No, as adopted children they had their own unique DNA and it was fallible.

You see, for God to make Adam and Eve perfect, in His divine image, he had to design in a fatal flaw. That's not because He has a flaw, but rather because one of his most important characteristics couldn't be manifest in them, without the ability to deny that characteristic. You see, *"God is love"* (1 Jn 4:8) and to have the characteristic of love, one must have a free will. One must have the ability to choose not to love; otherwise, it is not love. Robots cannot love.

To make it possible for them to love, God gave Adam and Eve a free will, knowing that they would misuse it and bring pain, suffering and death into the world through their sin; and so they did. Eve listened to the serpent and accepted his words over those of God's. Adam, her husband, who scripture tells us was right there with her (Gen 3:6), didn't do a thing to stop her and in fact joined her in that sin.

So Adam and Eve sinned and thought them sin, death and corruption entered the world. While we could have a long discussion on that, and the effects of their sin, the only effect that matters to us at this moment is that we all inherited that sin nature. Like Adam and Eve, we have all been created with a fatal flaw, the same fatal flaw that they had.

But I'll have to say that it's even worse with us. You see, Adam and Eve were the best that God could create them to be. But somewhat more than 400 generations have passed since then.

Generations in which sin has taken a toll on mankind, corrupting us more and more. In fact, it got so bad at one point, that God decided that He had to destroy all mankind, except one pious family, headed by a man named Noah, and start over (Gen 6:5-8).

But that didn't allow God the opportunity to remove the fatal flaw in mankind. He had to leave it there, or they couldn't love Him; and more than anything, he wanted children who loved Him, as much as He loved them. So the fatal flaw remained.

Just like the first time, it didn't take long for the fatal flaw to assert itself and for Noah's descendents to sin. The bloodline of man started down the road to corruption once again. Yet this time, it had a head start, because Noah and his sons weren't as perfect as Adam and Eve had been. Sin and corruption multiplied across the face of the earth, just as fast as man could fill it.

It has been more than 4,300 years since Noah and his sons stepped out of the ark. Since that day, each generation which has been born has built upon the actions of the generation before. In some cases that was for good, as mankind developed new and better ways of doing things. But in at least as many ways, it was bad, as we can see that each generation has been moving farther and farther from our Heavenly Father, while we have been moving farther and farther into sin.

You and I were born into a sinful world, and born with a sin nature. So was your spouse. As it says in Romans 3:10, "... *There is none righteous, no not one.*" Nor are there any of us who are perfect. We; you, I and your spouse, are all imperfect beings, born into an imperfect world, raised by imperfect parents and taught how to live and love by an imperfect society.

We already talked about how babies prove our imperfection and our true, selfish nature. Yes, babies are cute and lovable, and it's a good thing they re. Otherwise, we probably wouldn't take care of them. Yet they are self-centered; as far as they are concerned, the baby is king and all must bow to the merest wish of the baby. Waaa!

Yes, babies are all born with the ability to make us jump, even better than a drill sergeant can make a platoon of green recruits jump when he yells. But sadly, the baby, like the drill sergeant, thinks that this is a normal state and that things should continue that way. While the drill sergeant is correct in his assessment, the baby is not. One day, they have to learn that they really aren't king and they really don't have the ability to command everyone to obey.

That's a hard lesson to learn, especially when you consider that in the baby's experience, that is the norm. It's truly heartbreaking when their reign of terror comes to an end. But fortunately, babies hearts heal quickly and they slowly begin to learn that life without being king can still be pretty good.

But that's not all the baby has to learn. You see, babies are savages. They don't know how to behave. They do what feels good at the moment, without any thought of consequence. Sadly, like their royal crown, their savagery must be eliminated. Another hard lesson... or a thousand.

Any parent can tell you that a child left alone, without rules or instruction, will destroy anything they can get their hands on. This is part of their savagery that must be removed from them. They need to learn how to take care of things, how to use them properly, and how to prevent from being hurt by the things around them. They also need to learn how to interact with others, including such hard lessons as having to share their toys. It's hard being a toddler.

That's why God created the family. Children need parents to train and guide them. Otherwise, all they will learn is how to do wrong. It seems that when children teach other children, that is all they are able to teach.

Eventually, all children learn; at least those with loving parents who take the time and effort to train and discipline them. Those without such parents often end up populating our prison system, as they never grow out of being savages. They must be removed from society, in order to stop them from hurting others around them.

Actually, if we look at the whole situation, it's much worse than that. What I mean is that we aren't just born into an imperfect world, but a world full of sin. As such, society literally teaches us how to sin. It doesn't teach us how to be godly and righteous, which would be useful, it teaches us to follow in its pattern, which is one of sin.

This is the world your spouse was born into. Like everyone else, they were born with a sin nature. They were savages who had to be tamed. But while some were working to tame them, others were teaching them how to sin. Rather than being made perfect, they were being made more and more imperfect.

Some even took it a step farther, causing pain in the life of your spouse as they grew and matured. That pain has left scars on their heart, many of which have never properly healed. Those scars cause them to react in what might seem like illogical or irrational ways; but are probably defensive in nature. The pain they have felt is real and they can't afford to feel it again.

The person you married isn't a perfect work of art. Rather, their inner beauty is in spite of what the world has done to them, rather than because of it. Whatever good is in them has been placed there by God Himself, through His Holy Spirit. The rest? That came from the world.

You are no better; you're just as flawed and imperfect as they are. For every flaw you can see in your spouse, you have one too. Maybe it's not the same flaw, but you can rest assured that it is as deep, as wide and as serious as the one they are showing to you.

What's wrong with your spouse is that they are an imperfect person, born into an imperfect world. They are trying to overcome it, but at times they feel like they are overwhelmed by the imperfections. You know that feeling, for you have felt it too. At times they lash out at you, because they don't know what to do; and at times you lash out at them, for the very same reason. Both of you are struggling to overcome and also to become what God has created you to be.

God is at work in your spouse, taking that broken pot that you married and binding up the wounds. He's pouring in salve and ointment, bringing healing. Some day, he will be able to take off the dressing, and let the perfect vessel come to light. But it's a slow process, often one that takes our entire lives.

So what should you do with this imperfect person that you married? You should love them and give them grace. Learn how to forgive and how to accept their little foibles. Learn how to overlook their failings and laugh with them when they make a mistake. But more than anything, you must learn to give them grace. Permit them to be the imperfect person that they are, and love them because of it, not just in spite of it.

Action Items:

- Repent of expecting perfection from your spouse, when you aren't able to display it yourself.
- Learn to celebrate the victories that your spouse has over their carnal nature, encouraging them for every little bit of godliness you see in their lives.
- Try to rediscover the scars on your spouse's heart and start praying for them to be healed.

5

Voices in Your Head

All of us struggle from time to time with negative thoughts about our spouses; some of us, more than others. Those thoughts just seem to come unbidden, even when we're trying to stop ourselves from thinking that way. But after some time, we just seem to find it easier to see the negative in them and focus on that, than we do to see the good in them and focus on that.

Have you ever wondered where those thoughts come from? Have you ever thought perhaps that they were not your own thoughts? Could it be that someone is actually putting those thoughts into your head, trying to get you thinking poorly about your spouse, for the purpose of destroying your marriage?

I know it sounds kind of crazy and like I'm trying to make it sound like you belong in a loony bin somewhere, but let's just suppose for a moment, that those voices are not your own. Yeah, I'm saying that you're hearing voices; but don't worry, I'm hearing them too.

Please don't close the book. Give me time to explain. We all know that one of the archangels, Lucifer, fell from grace when he declared that he wanted to take over God's position (Is 14:13-14). That was probably the shortest rebellion in history, as Jesus said, *"I behind Satan as lightning fall from heaven"* (Lk 10:18). Sadly though, he took a third of the angels in heaven with him in his ill-begotten rebellion.

Lucifer is now known as Satan and the angles who fell with him are known as demons. While still retaining some of the characteristics of their former glory, their character has been turned to evil. As such, they serve Satan, attempting to destroy God's greatest creation, the children of Adam.

One of the ways in which they do that is by messing with our thoughts. I've said for years that the biggest battle that any Christian faces is the one between their left ear and their right ear. You know, where all that grey matter resides. The battle we have to win, before we can even think of winning any other, it's the battle over our thought life.

That's why Satan's little demons like to mess with our thoughts. Each of us have demons assigned to us, which are commonly referred to as "familiar spirits." They are familiar because they are familiar with us. Actually, they are somewhat more familiar with us, than we are with ourselves. You see, these spirits have the job of becoming experts in the person they are assigned to. They study our reactions to the world around us, especially those who are closest to us, noting how things affect us.

You see, these spirits are looking for our weaknesses. They want to know what will illicit ungodly behavior from us. Specifically, they want to know our hot buttons, triggers and anything else that can cause us to act the way the devil wants us to act, and not the way that God wants us to act.

That's dangerous. These spirits know us so well, that they can manipulate us into doing just about anything they want... unless we stop them. But to stop them, we have to recognize that they are there. That's not easy to do, because they speak to us, speaking directly into our minds, in the first person, so it sounds like our own thoughts. We don't recognize the thought as being something from outside of ourselves, so we accept it and keep going along in the same vein.

Let me assure you, the thoughts they are putting into our heads are not about the women's sewing circle or the men's bowling club. They're thoughts intended to make us fall into sin, in one way or another. That doesn't necessarily mean going out and robbing a bank or committing adultery, it could very well mean thinking negatively about your spouse.

The struggles that led to me writing this book started about ten years ago, during a time when I went thought an entire year of emotional crisis. Yes, an entire year; or if you hear my wife say anything about it, more than a year. It was a difficult time, but it was also a time when I learned much.

I talked about this in the forward, but allow me to repeat myself, as it is important to this chapter. At that time, we had been living in a motorhome for nine years. For some reason, my city girl wife was tired of that and wanted to move into a house. There was just one little problem; we didn't have any money. We were working as missionaries along the Texas/ Mexico border and living off the offerings we received. So, she asked me if it was okay with me for her to go back to work teaching, so that we could have enough money to rent a house.

Even though I didn't like the idea, knowing that she would be a teacher 24/7 and not have time for other things, I went alone. As I had quietly predicted, once she started working, she didn't have time for the ministry, didn't have time for the family, and didn't have time for me. I had a wife for 20 minutes a day, while we ate dinner (which I prepared). The rest of the time she was awake, she was either at school or grading papers at home.

That's when I went into an emotional nosedive and I had lots of help doing it too. Remember those familiar spirits I was talking about a moment ago? Well, they started talking to me. They told me all sorts of things like, "She doesn't love me." "She doesn't want anything to do with me." "She cares more about those kids at school, than she does me." "She just wants me to do things for her, she doesn't want me." "She has time for everything else, but not for me." And on and on, ad nauseam.

It was like a broken record, repeating the same garbage to be over and over, all day long. I found myself almost constantly offended at my wife, from the time I woke up in the morning, to the time I went to bed at night.

It wasn't that my wife was doing anything wrong; she was just working too much. She is a very good teacher and she was very dedicated to her work. But teachers, at least good teachers, work hard and work a lot of hours. She worked so hard that she didn't have time for much of what she had been doing before. That wasn't her fault; it was the nature of the job she was doing.

But that didn't stop the enemy from using it against me. He had a hook in me and he was reeling in a big catch. His constant negative statements were really doing a number on me, one that I hope to never live through again.

Don't get me wrong here; I'm not talking about possession, but rather oppression. There's a huge difference between the two. Possession is when the spirit is inside the person, controlling them. Oppression is when the spirit is outside the person, talking to them. But like I said, it talks in the first person, so we think it's our own words.

The easiest way to imagine it is this. Remember when you were a kid, watching the Saturday morning cartoons? Some cartoon character or other had to make a decision and a *poof* a little devil showed up on one side of his head, talking to him and telling him to do bad. Then another *poof* and a little angel showed up on the other side, telling him to do good. That demon showing up and talking to the cartoon character is oppression, and you and I face it every day.

It took me several months to figure out what was going on with me. I honestly thought that those were my own thoughts. So, like anyone else, I went along for the ride... only it wasn't a very fun ride. Finally I got tired of it and tried to get off, but the thoughts kept coming. They even came when I was trying to think positive thoughts about my wife. That's when I started to realize what was going on.

The devil loves to work in the dark, where nobody can see what he's up to. But once he's exposed to the light, it's a whole lot harder for him to keep playing his games. Once I realized that the thoughts that I was hearing were not my own, I knew it was time to take action. I even knew what the Bible had to say about it.

> *For although we walk in the flesh, we do not war after the flesh. 4 (For the weapons of our warfare are not carnal, but mighty though God to the pulling down of strongholds.) 5 Casting down imaginations, and every high thing that exalteth itself against the knowledge of God, and bringing into captivity every thought to the obedience of Christ.*
>
> *2 Corinthians 10:3-5*

There's the key, casting down those imaginations and bringing our thoughts into captivity, making both act in obedience to Christ.

Let me break that down. First, I have to be acting in obedience to Christ, so that I can appropriate His authority. Then, once I've got myself straight, the next step is to cast down the imaginations. In other words, refuse the image that those negative statements are giving me about my wife. Finally, I need to take my thoughts captive. That means that I take control of my thoughts, no longer letting those familiar spirits put thoughts into my mind. That's God's instructions in the matter.

I won't say it was easy and I won't say it wasn't a battle. But it was a battle I won. It took time, but I learned how to cast down those imaginations and take my thoughts captive. I stopped allowing those devils to put thoughts in my mind and just accepting them. That doesn't mean that they don't still try, they do. But now, I recognize those thoughts for what they are and don't accept them.

Actually, there were days when I fought that battle 50 times or more, in the same day. But fight I did. One of the weapons I used was forgiveness and another was praise. I'll talk more about those in another chapter.

In other words, in the battle between my left ear and my right ear, I have become the victor. That doesn't mean that I never have another battle crop up. But now I understand how to win them. So, while the enemy might take ground for a moment, I eventually end up winning, all over again.

Few believers ever win this battle, because few ever realize what is happening to them. They don't recognize the enemy's work in their thoughts, thinking that it is just themselves. That could be one of the greatest lies the enemy has ever told; and it's one he tells to everyone.

Don't allow yourself to dwell in negative thoughts about your spouse. When those negative thoughts come around, kick them out! Demand that they go and they must flee. But here's the other part; replace them with good thoughts. Don't allow yourself to sit there with your mind on neutral, or those thoughts will come right back to haunt you. You've got to fill that space with something, and it had better be something positive.

If you're having trouble thinking positive thoughts about your spouse at the moment, then think positive thoughts about Jesus. Let your mind dwell in His Word. Thank Him for all the great things He has done for you. Worship Him. Do something. That way, when the spirits come back to hassle you again, they won't find you just waiting for them.

Action Items:

- Start questioning your own thoughts, especially the negative ones and the ones that tempt you to sin. Are they truly your thoughts or are you merely accepting those thoughts that are being handed to you?
- Reject ungodly thoughts, "casting them down" by refusing to accept them. It helps to declare this out loud, stating that you do not accept such-and-such a thought.
- Develop the habit of turning the tables on those negative thoughts, instantly replacing them with positive thoughts.

6

WHAT'S IN YOUR HEART?

There are deep, dark places in the world, where only the brave dare to go. They are filled with snares and pitfalls for the unwary, those who wander in unexpected. For this reason, few are willing to tread those paths. Oh, they talk about what's in there and they act like they have intimate knowledge of those dark places; but what they're really talking about is the shallower places; those that are easily accessible and where light can still get in.

Even the things found in those shallower places can be pretty scary, especially when they are loosed on the unprepared. That often happens quickly and explosively, without warning. The explosions come because those places are unstable, easily tipped out of balance by seemingly insignificant things.

I am talking, of course, about the heart. Many of us have things hidden in the dark recesses of our hearts, which are better left unsaid. Yet those things are often saved, like prized treasures, more because we don't know what to do about them, than for any other reason. Yet because they are there, they affect our thoughts, feelings, attitudes and actions.

Perhaps I've gotten you confused, but the heart can be a pretty confusing thing. That's because the heart works on so many different levels. We find in scripture that the heart is referred to on a spiritual basis, on an emotional basis and on a physical basis. That makes it the nexus that connects the three parts of man; body, soul and spirit.

But the heart goes even beyond that in complexity, because it is capable of being divided into an infinite number of separate areas. Things in one area of the heart may be connected to other areas of the heart, or they may be totally isolated, on their own.

Much of that has to do with how the things that are in our heart got there in the first place. Those things which entered in our hearts through traumatic or emotional circumstances generally have the greatest domain, being firmly planted and connected to unforgettable memories. The mind might try to block those memories, placing them behind a wall, but that's as dangerous a trap as those found in the heart. Those memories can spring out from behind the wall at any time. All they need is the right trigger.

Each of us is thoroughly connected to our past, where all those memories and all the hidden things in the dark recesses of our hearts came from. Oh, we may try to pretend that they don't exist, but that only works until they rear their ugly heads and let us know that they are still there.

What that means is that all of our thoughts, actions and reactions are affected to some extent by our past. This isn't something that just some of us deal with. It's not just limited to people who have been raped or abused. It's something we all deal with. We all have a past and we are all affected by it; sometimes in rather difficult ways.

So when your spouse says or does something, it isn't just the you of today that's responding to them, but the you of a year ago, five years ago, ten years ago and even the five year old you that's still there inside.

Rarely will the old you have anything good to offer you, to help you react in a positive way. That's because those old versions of you tend to have much stronger memories of the bad, then they have of the good. The strong negative emotions associated with those memories burn them deeper into our minds and hearts, where they are always available to us. Yet the positive memories are not so well engraved, simply because they don't have the same strong emotional attachment.

What this all means is that we often react to our spouse, not based on what they have said or done, but rather, what has been done to us by others in our past. The easiest place to see this is in someone who has been divorced and remarried. Those people tend to expect their second spouse to be like their first. Therefore, they're going to expect them to have the same reactions, the same bad habits and the same problems that their first spouse did.

But this doesn't just apply to those who have been remarried. It applies equally to all of us. Each person we have known in our lives and each experience we have had has affected us in some way or other. That can be good or it can be bad, all depending on the person, what they've done, and how we reacted to it.

The deeper and longer any relationship is, the more of an affect it has on us. That's why people who have been married before will be carrying a lot of emotional baggage from their first marriage. It's not the fact that they had a wedding or a piece of paper that says that they were married or divorced, it's the length of time they were in relationship with each other and how deeply emotional the relationship was.

Of course, not all relationships are equal; not even all marriage relationships. Some have highly emotional marriages, while others have much less emotional involvement. Even within the relationship itself, one party might have a strong emotional bond to the other, which is not fully reciprocated.

So this means that we must understand that our reactions to our spouses are flawed from the outset. None of us react perfectly or are even capable of reacting perfectly, no matter how hard we might try.

With that being the case, why would we blame our spouses for the way we interpret their words and actions? What makes us so sure that they are the ones in the wrong? Could it be that it's much easier to cast the blame on them, than it is to accept the fact that we could be the one at fault and be forced to look at those deep, dark places in our hearts?

Yet, as long as we put off dealing with what's in our own hearts, we are incapable of truly reacting correctly to our spouse. Oh, we might act correctly at times or even most of the time; but we won't be able to react correctly to them when they hit our hot buttons. That's where the problem is.

You know about those hot buttons. We all have them. Some of us have them well protected, so that nobody can find them. But others have them standing out in the open, with a big red sign pointing them out. Either way, when they get hit, it transforms us from Doctor Jekyll to Mister Hyde. The inner monster comes out and it's thirsty for blood.

Sadly, it is our spouses who bear the brunt of Mister Hyde's tirades. The closest person to us and the most important person in our lives, besides Jesus, is the one who feels the wrath of that monster. Whether it is expressed through violence, yelling, denying our spouse something they need from us, or giving the other person the silent treatment, it's all the same. What leaves us and goes to them is pain, hurt and anger, not love.

This is something that needs to be changed. We can't change our spouse, but we all have the opportunity to change ourselves. We may not think we have the ability, but we do have the opportunity. Ability is another thing, and fortunately, we don't have to depend on our own.

If we can actually take a moment to be honest with ourselves, we'd realize that our hearts need a good housecleaning. We need to clear out the cobwebs, wipe off the dust and especially get rid of the bad memories and the negative feelings associated with them. Unfortunately, that's not all that easy to do. Perhaps that's why so few people try.

But here's the important thing, we don't have to do this on our own. We have the help of one who is an expert in turning old stuff into new stuff (2 Cor 5:17). He is the original healer, and the one who created us as well. And He is the only one who is able to heal a wounded heart. Doctors can't, psychologists can't, your pastor can't. But the Holy Spirit of God can.

Here's the key though. The Holy Spirit won't be able to accomplish a single change in us, without our active participation. We have to desire the change and be willing to put up with the pain of surgery. But if we are willing, he is gentle and patient to perform that heart surgery, removing the pain, bitterness and sadness from each and every wound that is in there. Then he puts in new tissue, making our hearts new once again.

The first step is that we have to gain an understanding of what it is that need to change in us. That means honestly looking at ourselves and our reactions to our spouse, with an eye towards seeing what is wrong with us. That's not easy.

It helps to have someone on the outside, someone that you trust, who has the wisdom to look at you and the courage to tell you the truth. You may not like what they say, but *"faithful are the wound of a friend"* (Prov 27:6a).

The other one who can show us what needs to change in our hearts is the Holy Spirit. But we have to ask Him to show us that. He won't do it otherwise. Then, we have to be willing to accept what he shows us. That's even harder. We are so accustomed to making excuses for ourselves and justifying our actions, that our automatic reaction to what the Holy Spirit shows us will be to follow that pattern. After all, accepting who we really are isn't anywhere near as easy as blaming our spouse.

Once we accept what the Holy Spirit shows us, we need to ask Him to change us. Once again, He won't do anything unless we ask, nor will he do it unless we are active participants. That means that our part is to make every effort to not react in the way that we have reacted before, while He makes the permanent changes deep down in our hearts, which will get rid of the desire to react in those ways.

The Holy Spirit is capable of changing anything we need changed. He really is. And He will do it in a way that we won't even realize it is happening. But one day, we'll wake up to the fact that we are not reacting as we did before; that something has been done in us, and a part of our heart has been renewed.

Please keep in mind that this is not a one-time thing. Asking the Holy Spirit to take something bad out of us and turn it into something good doesn't mean that He will do everything. No, He'll work on one thing at a time, or maybe two. Then He will wait until we are hungry for Him to do more.

Action Items:

- Go to your spouse and apologize to them for all the times when you're reacted inappropriately to them, due to things out of your past. You don't need to be specific, unless something specific comes to your mind; make it general.
- Develop the habit of stopping yourself, when you find yourself getting angry and ask yourself the question, "What is truly causing the problem, is it them or something from my past?"
- As those things from your past which are causing negative reactions are revealed, write them down. Then actively seek for healing in those areas. This may require going to your pastor for counseling.
- Ask the Holy Spirit to show you the dark things hidden in your heart. In fact, make that a habit.

7

WHAT'S GOD DOING TO ME?

It is widely recognized in the Body of Christ that God's number one priority in our lives is that we come to the saving knowledge of Jesus Christ. But what about after that? If that was His only goal in our lives, wouldn't it make more sense to take us to heaven as soon as we got saved, before we could backslide and end up in sin? Yet God leaves us here on this Earth, for however many more years we have.

Obviously, at least some of us would need to stay here in order to evangelize and win more people to Christ. But while the Great Commission calls us all to spread the gospel, we are not all evangelists. God didn't create us all that way, because there are other things to do. There are many more needs than the act of salvation.

God doesn't leave us here just to do His work upon the Earth either, although that is enough of a reason in and of itself. God leaves us here so that He can use the circumstances of our lives to change us. "Change us into what?" you might ask. Change us into the image of His Son.

> *For whom He did foreknow, He also did predestine to be conformed to the image of His Son, that He might be the firstborn among many brethren.*
>
> *Romans 8:29*

This is God's number one goal in our lives, once we are saved.

His love towards us is so great, that He is unwilling to leave us in the imperfect state that He finds us in. That's why He sent His Son. The salvation which we receive is much more than just the right to go to heaven, it's the right to have our whole lives redeemed and made into something better, and He will use whatever He has to, in order to make that happen.

The process of change is often difficult. For this reason, most of us enter into this process kicking and screaming. We don't want to change, even if it is into something better and is ultimately for our benefit. God knows this and is patient with us. Much more patient, I might add, than we are with ourselves.

It would help if we had some idea of what God is trying to change us into. We find that, in Romans 8:29, which we just read. It shows us that His goal is to change us into the image of His Son, Jesus Christ.

That doesn't mean that we stop being ourselves or stop having our own personality. God likes variety. He even likes the people that we are, each of us an individual. What He doesn't like is the ways in which we fall short of being the kinds of people that He created us to be, with the kind of character that He intended for us to have. In other words, we fall short in our humanity, especially the carnal part of it.

We must always remember that one of the gifts that God has given us is a free will. He had to do that, so that we could choose to love Him or reject Him; obey Him or go our own way; live the life that He wants us to enjoy or fail and merely live a carnal life, grubbing for the little that this world has to offer.

So, what God wants us to do, is to willingly give up the parts of our character that are destructive to ourselves and those around us, so that we can receive the character of Christ and be like Him. That doesn't mean that we stop being ourselves, but rather that we manifest the character of Christ through our own distinct personality. It's not so much about the personality that we have, as it is about the character that we possess.

So where do we find the character of Christ written out for us in the Bible? In a sense, we could say that the whole Bible talks about that. But if we want the short version, we need look no further than Galatians, chapter 5:

> *But the fruit of the Spirit is love, joy, peace, longsuffering, gentleness, goodness, faith, 23 meekness, temperance: against such there is no law.*
>
> *Galatians 5:22-23*

This is a very key verse in our Bibles, yet it is one that way too many believers merely gloss over. More than anything, it is used as a teaching for children in Sunday School, where they color some pictures of fruit and make mobiles out of them. It is rarely preached and even more rarely studied in depth.

Yet this verse describes the fullness of the character that God is trying to mold into each and every one of us. These are our spiritual organs, and just like a newborn baby has a small heart and small lungs, when we are born again we have a small love, a small faith and all of the other spiritual organs on a small scale. To mature and become Christ-like as we are supposed to, these nine character traits, our spiritual organs, must grow within us to become strong and steadfast.

When we look at the carnal nature we are born with, this seems almost to be an insurmountable task. None of us readily develop these traits on our own, but only with the help of the Holy Spirit. But how does the Holy Spirit do that, does He just reach inside us and make them grow, without our participation or knowledge of what is happening?

Absolutely not. If the fruit of the Spirit is going to grow in us, it can only happen with our active participation. That's the part we may not like. If we need more patience, He gives us circumstances which allow patience to grow within us. If we need more faith, He gives us circumstances in which we have to use our faith. If we need more love, He gives us people to love, even people who we may not feel are all that loveable.

All of this happens either through the events and situations in our lives or the people we come into contact with. Each and every person in our lives is there for a purpose, perhaps even more than one purpose. One of those is going to be to help us to change into the people we need to be.

Quite simply God places people and circumstances in our lives, which show the need for us to change. We then have the choice of staying the way we are, or becoming what God wants us to be. While many choose to stay the same, even in the Body of Christ, they are only hurting themselves. They are losing much of the blessing that God has for them.

If all we do is complain about the people that God has placed in our lives, then we are saying that we will not change. We are demanding that others change to accommodate us. Let me get a little more personal about that. When all we do is complain about our spouse, we are saying that we are fine and our spouses are the ones with the problems. But in reality, each and every thing that we are complaining about shows something that needs work on in us.

That's not to say that they don't have a problem, it's just recognizing that we do too. Our problem is that we are not yet remade into the image of Jesus Christ. Being forced to deal with that other person's problem is helping to remake us, more specifically, it's helping to manifest the fruit of the Spirit in our lives.

In other words, the person that you are having so much trouble with was custom picked by God, to show you where you need to change. They keep hitting your hot buttons, because you need them hit. Otherwise, you'll allow your problems to stay there, hidden away, and never deal with them.

The greatest tool which the Holy Spirit has available to Him, in this effort to show us where the fruit of the Spirit is not yet manifest in our lives, is our spouse. That is the closest relationship that any of us have. As such, it is the one which is going to reveal the most about our inner person, no matter how hard we try to hide it.

Our spouses are able to see right through us, knowing when something is going on inside. They may not know exactly what is going on, but they will definitely recognize that something is. Even more than that, they know exactly where our buttons are. If we ever need to have our buttons pushed, they are the ones best equipped to do the job.

That's obviously not what we thought we were getting married for on our wedding day. But it is part of what God had in mind. He was looking for a person who would help to complete us, and part of that process is to help us become more like Jesus. That requires getting the old us out, so the new us can come in and take over.

For the old us to get out, it has to manifest. That way, we can be made aware of what's really inside us. In turn, that awareness gives us a choice. We either accept things as they are, or we decide to become part of the change process.

Accepting things as they are has a price. It means that things will never get better. We'll continue having the same issues with our spouse, the same problems in our marriage and the same things irritating us and dragging us down. Is that what you want for the rest of your life?

"Yeah, but it's their fault" you might say. Yes, part of it is. They are doing things that they shouldn't be doing. But part of it is your fault too. You are doing things you should be either. You're also reacting to them in ways that you shouldn't, and that's the part that the Holy Spirit wants you to see. He wants you to see it and be sickened by it, so that you'll become an active participant in the change that He's trying to bring about in you.

Action Items:

- Repent to God for your stubbornness in not allowing the Holy Spirit to change you.
- Begin to work on growing the fruit of the Spirit in your life. Pick one fruit to start with and work on it. After a while, change to another. Continue in this way, returning for more work on individual fruit, as needed. This should continue your whole life.
- Ask the Holy Spirit to help you manifest the fruit of the Spirit in your life.
- Learn to recognize when things that your spouse does bring forth the bad in you and ask the Holy Spirit to show you what those are.

8

Your Rights and Responsibilities in Marriage

As a minister, I've done my share of marriage counseling, seeing the best side of people and sometimes the worst side of the very same people. It's amazing how even the most pious looking people can turn into something quite different, when they're in a counseling session and trying to defend themselves.

One of the things these people regularly bring up in counseling sessions is their supposed "rights." I've heard people claim that they have a right to all sorts of things. Some of them are reasonable sounding things to expect out of their marriages and others that make we wonder about the sanity of the person declaring that right. Then there are some which are just out-and-out creepy.

I always wonder where these people get their ideas from, but I long ago stopped asking. There was no sense asking about something that didn't make sense anyway, as I found that the explanation they would supply didn't make any more sense.

Perhaps our fixation on rights comes from being an American. After all, no other country has our Constitution and Bill of Rights. We are a people fixated on those rights, to the point where new ones are being made up by every splinter group and special interest all the time. And just like the ones that people bring up in marriage counseling, many of those are loco too.

Our Bill of Rights exists because the Founding Fathers believed that God gave us those rights, not the government. That makes sense, because God created us. So if anyone would have the authority to give us rights, it would have to be God.

So I went to the source, in search of all the rights we had in marriage. I was sure there were some there, even something that I wasn't getting from my wife, which I had a right to receive. After a long and thorough search of scripture, I found that we have... absolutely... no... rights... whatsoever... in... our... marriages.

That's right; there isn't one single right mentioned in scripture, either for the husband or the wife. All these things that people were trying to tell me were "their rights" were nothing more than figments of their imaginations. Somehow or other they had gotten the idea that something they wanted was a right, and they've been beating their spouse over the head with it for years.

Men, you don't have a right to sex, no matter how much you think you do. Women, you don't have a right for your husband to meet your emotional needs. Neither of you have a right to expect the other person to make you happy. God didn't give you those rights, he gave you responsibilities.

Focusing on the things you think are your marital rights is self-centered. In other words, it's the opposite of loving your spouse. Rather than loving them, it is, in a sense, demanding that they love you. Not only that, but it is demanding that they love you in a specific way, regardless of whether that is their love language or not. You are making it clear that you don't care about them; all you care about is that you receive what you want, when you want it.

Hmm, sounds a lot like a spoiled child, doesn't it?

True love requires that we give to the other person, not receive from them. Yes, it's always nice to receive, but if you are demanding what you want, then what you will receive will not come out of love, it will come out of fear of your reaction if they deny you. There's no love in that sort of marital blackmail. You aren't giving love, nor are you receiving it either.

What if we could turn the tables on that a bit? You've probably heard the saying sometime that marriage is a 50/50 relationship. Well, it's not. If all you're giving is 50%, then you're obviously breaking your marriage vows. You're cheating your spouse out of what you promised to give them. Your spouse didn't marry you to only receive half, any more than you married them so that you could receive half. Both of you need to be giving your all to the marriage and each other.

That's what I mean by turning the tables. What would happen to your marriage, if you stopped worrying about receiving from your spouse and started concentrating on giving to them? Better yet, what if both of you started thinking that way; how much would that change things?

If you could both concentrate on acting that way towards each other, you could literally transform your marriage. No longer would it be a contest to see who can get the most from the other one, it would become a contest to see who could bless the other one the most. You know the nice thing about that contest? Both of you win.

So, how do we know what we are supposed to give to our spouse? The Bible tells us. There are a number of passages of scripture, which clearly identify our marital responsibilities. Even if we did nothing else, just completing with those things would be huge. It would turn your marriage into something totally new.

Lets' take a look at a few key passages:

> *Love is patient, love is kind. It does not envy, it does not boast, it is not proud. [5] It is not rude, it is not self-seeking, it is not easily angered, it keeps no record of wrongs. [6] Love does not delight in evil but rejoices with the truth. [7] It always protects, always trusts, always hopes, always preserves. [8] Love never fails.*
>
> *I Corinthians 13:4-8a*

> *Wives submit yourselves unto your own husbands, as unto the Lord. [23] For the husband is the head of the wife, even as Christ is the head of the church: and he is the savior of the body. [24] Therefore, as the church is subject unto Christ, so let eh wives be to their own husbands in every thing. [25] Husbands, love your wives, even as Christ also loved the church, and gave himself for it; [26] That he might sanctify and cleanse it with the washing of water by the word, [27] That he might present it to himself a glorious church, not having spot, or wrinkle, or any such thing; but that it should be holy and without blemish.*
>
> *Ephesians 5:22-27*

> *But since there is so much immorality, each man should have his own wife, and each woman her own husband. [3] The husband should fulfill his marital duty to his wife, and likewise the wife to her husband. [4] The wife's body does not belong to her alone but alos to her husband. In the same way, the husband's body*

does not belong to him alone but also to his wife. [5] *Do not deprive each other except by mutual consent and for a time, so that you may devote yourselves to fasting and prayer. Then come together again, so that Satan will not tempt you because of your lack of self-control.*

1 Corinthians 7:2-5 NIV

For after this manner in the old time the holy women also, who trusted in God, adorned themselves, being in subjection unto their own husbands: [6] *Even as Sara obeyed Abraham, calling him lord: whose daughters ye are, as long as ye do well, and are not afraid with any amazement.* [7] *Likewise, ye husbands, dwell with them according to knowledge, giving honour unto the wife, as unto the weaker vessel, and as being heirs together of the grace of life; that your prayers be not hindered.*

1 Peter 3:5-7

These are by no means anywhere near all the verse in the Bible that talk about marriage. But they are some of the key ones that point out what we are supposed to do in marriage. That's why I picked them.

Now that you've read those verses, I want you to go back and read them again. But this time, rather than picking out what your spouse should be doing for you (we all tend to do that), I want you to focus on the things you are supposed to do for them. Those are your responsibilities.

Interestingly enough, when God gives a responsibility to one marriage partner, He doesn't give the other partner a corresponding right. Rather, He just tells that other partner their responsibility as well.

Let me give you an example of what I mean by that. I'll use one of the historically misused points about marriage mentioned in those verses. That is, where it tells women to submit to their husbands. For centuries, men have used that as a license to subjugate their wives, forcing them to obey. But there are three problems with that.

- First of all, subjugation and submission aren't the same thing. Submission is an act of one's own will, while subjugation is forced on the other person.

- Secondly, submission and obedience aren't the same either. Submission is an attitude, while obedience is an action. It is possible to be submitted, without obeying, such as when the individual doesn't know how to do the task.

- Finally, there is nowhere in scripture where God tells men they have a right to subjugate their wives. It tells them to love their wives, as Christ loved the church.

It's time for us all to stop focusing on our rights and start focusing on our responsibilities. Until we do, we're going to live in a constant state of marital strife. We will expend a huge amount of energy trying to receive what we want and convince our spouse that they should give it to us.

Not only that, we are going to be constantly dissatisfied by our marriage, by our spouse, and by life in general. People who are so inwardly focused that all they can see is what they're not receiving are always miserable. But people who are focused outwardly, looking for ways to be a blessing to others, are always happy.

When we focus on receiving from our spouse, we will make

them feel used, rather than cherished; taken advantage of, rather than blessed; and unloved, rather than loved. Is that the type of message we want to be sending? Is that the way we want our spouse to act towards us?

But when we focus on giving to our spouse, we make them feel cherished, blessed and loved. They then, will begin to respond in kind, seeking ways to bless us and give us the love that we need. We may very well end up receiving the very thing that we wanted, but in this case, it will be given out of love, which will make is so much better.

I have stated before that there is no way that we can change our spouses, and I don't take that back in the least. But there is one way in which we can influence their actions, and this is it. The more loved that we can make them feel, the more they are going to want to love us in return.

Action Items:

- Make a vow to give all of yourself to your spouse, being a blessing to them, regardless of what they do to or for you. If you are studying this book together, make a joint commitment to each other to do that.
- Study the verses in the Bible that talk about marriage, seeking to understand your role and responsibilities. Work to fulfill those.

9

YEAH, BUT THEY...

All too many marriages take on the appearance of a medieval town square. You see people haggling back and forth, trading chickens, pigs and homegrown produce. Each wanting to make sure that they got a good deal out of the trade. If they can't come to an agreement that satisfies both parties, than the deal is off; but if they can, then everyone leaves at least somewhat happy.

Just how is that like a marriage relationship? Simple; in most marriages, each of the partners is trying to do whatever they can, to get all they can. They aren't really concerned about giving whatever they can to their spouse, except in the sense of trading something their spouse wants from them, for something they want from their spouse. The marriage relationship ends up turning into a constant stream of negotiations, with each seeking the advantage.

This doesn't usually happen on a verbal level, but on a non-verbal one. The two don't actually sit across a table from each other, with the man agreeing to take his wife on two dates for every time they have sex. Rather, it boils down to withholding what the other person wants, if we haven't received what we want.

You've probably heard the classic line, "If momma ain't happy, ain't nobody happy" and its cousin, "Happy wife, happy life." Both of these statements are based upon what I'm saying here. They are both a threat and a promise to the husband, that he had better make his wife happy. If he does, then everything will be okay; but if he doesn't, there will be hell to pay.

I'll have to say that women actually have the upper hand in these non-verbal negotiations. They've got something their husband wants, which he can't get anywhere else, without being in sin. He doesn't have anything like that, which he can use to counter. So, women are much more likely to get what they want... at least at first.

But the idea of using that advantage quickly breaks down. It doesn't take long for most men to realize that they are being manipulated by their wives. Once they do, they stop playing the game; or I should say, they look for ways to put the minimum possible effort into the game, without either dying of sexual starvation or having their wives kill them when the fangs and claws come out. Once the man gets to that point, the game stops being fun for the woman.

Please don't get me wrong here. I'm not trying to get down on women. All that was, was an example. Men play the game as much as their wives do, trying to get the wife to do what they want, without having to "pay" too much to get it.

Of course, neither one will admit to what they are doing. If you try and ask them, the answer you'll get will be something like, "Yeah, but they..." It will always be the other one's fault; and if you go ask the other spouse, you'll get the same thing. Neither one is happy with the situation as it is, but neither one is willing to take responsibility for doing something to make it better.

The worst thing about this system is that it spirals downwards in a never-ending spiral that ends at the grave. That is, it does so unless one of the spouses decides to do something to change it. Someone has to be the one to take a chance, giving to their spouse, without expecting anything in return. When they do that, there is the opportunity for the spiral to reverse, and start going back up again.

Correct me if I'm wrong, but I don't remember anything in the marriage vows about either party saying that their commitment is dependent upon the other. Rather, the typical marriage vows talk about committing to the marriage, "for better, for worse, for richer, for poorer, in sickness and in health." That sounds pretty complete to me. Maybe the problem is that they forgot to put anything about being romantic, communicating and having sex in those vows.

Or maybe it's just that we don't understand what marriage really is. We all think we get married because we love the other person, when in fact we don't. What we really get married for is so that we can feel loved. That's a whole different thing.

You see, true love is all about giving. It's about meeting the other person's needs. It's about putting them first, before you. That's not really something that's within our nature. We are selfish creatures, who want what we want when we want it. The other people in our lives are there to give us those things; we aren't there to give them what they want.

Oh, we'll give them what they want all right. But only if they give us what we want. They, whichever they, have to go first. "Why should I do it, if they don't?" Sounds like a bunch of children, doesn't it?

But there's a worse part of this give and take too. That is, we justify our mistreatment of our spouse, on the mistreatment we've received from them. That's right. We think that if we feel mistreated, we have a right to make them feel the same... and we do it with gusto.

The classic example of this is a spouse that has an affair, to get even with their spouse, who already had an affair. Usually, the second partner doesn't have their affair until the first one is ended, the offending partner has confessed to their sin and some effort at restitution has been made. But then there's the price to be paid. The offended spouse decided that they have a right to get even, in the same way and to the same degree that they have been offended. After all, the Bible says, "an eye for an eye and a tooth for a tooth, doesn't it?"

Yes, Jesus referenced that in Matthew 5:38. But He wasn't agreeing with it. Rather, that's where he added, *"But I say to you, That ye resist not evil, but whosoever shall smite thee on thy right cheek, turn to him the other also"* (Matt 5:39). So it's clear that Jesus would not be in agreement with the actions of that offended spouse.

There are lots of different ways in which you can interpret that verse, but most Bible scholars agree that it's really not talking about physical blows, but rather offenses. In fact, it speaks directly to the situation I just raised up. Basically, it tells us that when our spouse has done wrong by us, we not only do not have a right to retaliate in kind, but that we should go so far as to give them the opportunity to do us wrong again.

How many times has each of us done wrong to the Lord? Yet we never reach a point where we have sinned against Him so many times, that His blood doesn't atone for our sins. No, each and every time we go back to Him in repentance, we are forgiven again, as if the sin had never happened.

That is a wonderful attribute of God and one that we could do well to emulate. The Bible tells us that he "throws our sins as far as the east is from the west" (Ps 103:12). Yet we remember all too well each and every transgression that our spouse has made against us and are way too quick to remind them when we feel that they are acting up again.

I learned some great marriage advice from a good friend of mine; something about how we should deal with each other, especially in times of dispute. That is, anything that is older than 30 days, doesn't exist. It can't be mentioned; it can't be used and we can't allow it to have any place in our heart. If it isn't important enough to deal with in those first 30 days, then it isn't important enough to deal with ever. Let it go.

Unfortunately, the human mind doesn't have the ability to willfully forget something. Oh, we forget plenty, but not because we decide to do so. Otherwise, we could choose to forget an offense, and it would be erased from our memory. How's that for a relational superpower?

Remember, those things that your spouse does, which you don't like; the offenses, are there for a purpose. They are there to show you what's wrong with your heart. God chose that spouse for you, so that you could grow more and more into the image of Christ.

That process might not be fun at times and it might even hurt. But it is for your good. Just like the body builders say at the gym, "No pain, no gain." Well, guess what, that applies to a whole lot more than just building muscle mass.

Everything your spouse does to hurt you will ultimately be used for your good. God promises us that in Romans 8:28. So even if it doesn't seem like it at the time, you can rest assured that God is going to make something good out of every bad thing that happens in your life, including every bad thing that someone else does to you.

So, what should you do in the meantime? How should you be reacting to the things that your spouse does, that push your buttons?

There is only one way you can react, which will bring glory to God; that is to love them with an everlasting, undying, unconditional love. As hard as it is and as impossible as it might seem, you are called by God to overcome evil with good (Rom 12:21). That includes all evil, of any kind, regardless of the source.

Think about that for a moment. If your spouse is doing something which you deem evil, what would happen if you overcame that evil with good? I'm not just talking about doing one or two good things, in spite of their actions. That wouldn't be overcoming the evil with your good. No, what I'm talking about is to treat them so good, that your goodness would put an end to their evil actions. Do you think you could do that?

You do realize, don't you, that if you were to do enough good towards your spouse, it would bring any evil they are doing to light... not in your eyes, but in theirs. It might take some time, but they would slowly start to realize that you have the moral high ground and they don't. That probably won't sit too well with them. They'll have to figure out a way to react; and while their first reaction might be to accuse you of doing something wrong, eventually they will have to turn to doing good as well, in order to keep themselves looking good in their own eyes.

So don't let "Yeah, but they..." be a part of your vocabulary. Rather, recognize that statement for what it is - self-centeredness in your own heart. Then, get rid of that self-centeredness and replace it with something better, something like the love of the Father.

Action Items:

- Make a vow to stop giving to your spouse only when they do what you want. Turn that around and decide to give the everything you can, no matter what they do.
- What thing is there that your spouse regularly wants you to do, that you don't? Start doing that daily to show your commitment to love them, no matter what.
- Is there anything you are doing to "retaliate" at your spouse? Make a decision to quit.

10

It Doesn't Matter What They Do

Once we get over the idea of our marriages being a barter system, where each only gives the other what they want, so that they can receive what they want in turn, it opens up a whole new world. That one decision frees us up from feeling as if we have to receive enough from our spouse, so that we are able to give in return. Rather, we can keep on giving, no matter what they do.

"Wait a minute," you might be thinking, "If I give up my expectation to receive from my spouse, who is going to make sure that my needs are met?"

That's actually a very valid question, even if the motivation behind it is one of those stinking things in our hearts. We all have needs and somehow or other those needs have to be fulfilled for us to be physically, emotionally, mentally and spiritually healthy. Of course, eating food, which fulfills a physical need, isn't going to fulfill our need to be close to God, which is a spiritual need. Neither is sleeping, which meets another physical need, going to fulfill our emotional need to feel loved.

In other words, we must find the right sort of provision to fulfill every need we have. Otherwise, that need goes unfulfilled. But what's to say that the source we are using to fulfill a certain need is the right source? Better yet, what if we're looking at the wrong source to fulfill our needs; what's that going to do to us?

Our bodies need nutrition to function and remain healthy. If we eat junk food all the time, we will be providing our bodies with food, but that food isn't going to be the right food to give our bodies nutrition. About all it will do is to give us energy, without the nutrients that we need to stay healthy. Those nutrients come from other types of food, definitely not junk food.

But what if we decided to start eating paper, grass and sawdust, instead of eating food; what would that do to us? Would it meet any of our body's needs for nutrition? Of course not. While a diet of paper, grass and sawdust might fill our stomachs and give us a sense of satisfaction, as if we were really eating, there would be nothing in it that would provide nourishment to our bodies. We could literally die with full bellies, because we were not filling them with food.

Okay, so where am I going with this? What would you say, if I were to say to you that you are expecting to receive something from your spouse, that they are not capable of giving you? Actually, we're expecting to receive a lot of things from our spouses, which we should be looking elsewhere for. But most specifically, we are looking to receive love (however we define it) from them, when we should be looking to God to give us love.

I know that sounds radical, but stick with me a moment. I can assure you that you need more love than your spouse can give you. We all do. That's just how we are. So what happens to us when we feel like we aren't getting the love that we need? We don't end up feeling "somewhat loved," or "partially loved," we end up feeling unloved.

This feeling of being unloved can even exist in a loving, giving marriage, simply because neither of the partners has enough love to give to the other, twenty-four hours a day, seven days a week, to fulfill their needs. There is always something that gets in the way; work, kids, money, the need to sleep, something.

But there is a source of love that is bottomless. That is God, or Heavenly Father. The apostle John tells us that "God is love" (1 John 4:16). That means that for all practical purposes, His love is infinite as well. When we come into relationship with Him, through Jesus Christ, we become recipients of that love. We suddenly have access to all the love we could ever need, and more.

That's supposed to be our source of love, not our spouse. Or rather, that's supposed to be the source that we look to in order to feel loved, rather than looking to our spouse. The fulfillment we need should come from our relationship with God, giving our love to Him and allowing Him to fill us to overflowing with his love. When we do that, we have more love than we need.

Sadly, very few Christians ever draw close enough to God to be filled with His love like this. Oh, they are willing to receive little dollop of His love, when they get saved. But they aren't willing to allow themselves to drown in the sea of His love. They aren't willing to become so overwhelmed by the love of God, that they just bask in His presence. Rather, they receive their little dollop of love and then go back to seeking love from their spouse, their friends, their kids and the other people in their lives.

Let me be extremely clear about this; our need for love is supposed to be fulfilled by God and no one else. That's not to say that we shouldn't receive love from anyone else; but that the love that we NEED comes from Him. Then, the love that we receive from others becomes the icing on the cake. Each little morsel becomes something precious and sweet; not just something to fulfill our needs.

When that happens, we appreciate the love that we receive from our spouses, rather than complaining that we aren't receiving enough. Each precious drop becomes a source of pleasure and we want to repay it. It literally transforms how we feel about them, through transforming how we feel about their love.

But there's another aspect of this as well, a very important one. That is, we can feel loved, even when our spouses do nothing at all. It won't matter what they do, because we are fulfilled. Our love tank is filled, so we aren't sucking them dry, trying to have them fill it up.

That allows us to act with love to them, in those times when they aren't able to act with love towards us. We all have times like that; times when we are sick, are suffering some emotional hurt, or are just having a bad day. Those are the times when we need love the most. We need the emotional healing power of love. We need every drop we can get.

This can become one of the true strengths of marriage. You see, if we are not dependent on our spouse to give us love, we are able to give them love in those times, without feeling a need to receive anything in return. We become a fountain of God's love, directed at the most important person in our lives.

This exact same concept applies to joy. Many of us look to our spouses to make us happy and we become bitter and upset when they don't. We somehow have the idea that one of the things that they promised to do for us was to make us happy. But nobody can truly make another person happy for long.

How many times has your spouse done something for you that made you happy? How long did that happiness last? Not long, right? Why is that? It's because we are depending on earthly happiness, rather than heavenly joy. The two are nothing alike, although they may seem alike in the moment when we are experiencing them.

True heavenly joy transcends our circumstances, while earthly happiness depends on them. That's why the happiness we receive from our spouses or the happiness we give to them doesn't last. Yet the joy we receive from our Heavenly Father can remain, regardless of what happens to us or around us. We can literally remain joyful through trials and suffering.

But for that to happen, we have to change our expectations. Rather than expecting our spouse to make us happy, which they can't really do, we have to learn how to receive the joy of the Lord. Doing that frees our spouses up from a huge responsibility that they can never hope to fulfill.

At the same time, just like being filled with God's love allows us to truly enjoy our spouse's love, being filled with God's joy allows us to truly enjoy the things that our spouses do to make us happy. The momentary happiness we received before won't just last a moment, but rather will become a warm glow that stays with us much longer. In some cases, it may actually become a part of us.

Okay, so now let's flip this over on the other side. What's going to happen to you, once you are filled with God's love and joy? How is that going to affect your actions and your attitude towards your spouse?

First of all, since you won't feel love starved, you won't have any reservations about giving your love to your spouse. Even in times when they aren't able to reciprocate, you will still be able to act in love. Not only that, but you will have an endless supply of that love to give them, because you won't be dependent on them filling your love tank back up. Your love will begin to become unconditional.

That's the sort of love we are supposed to have, one towards another; not the conditional kind that you find in most marriages. That conditional love is how the world loves, not how God loves. Since we are His children, made in His image and filled with His love, we should show that love at all times.

This means doing whatever you can, whenever you can, to fulfill your spouse's emotional needs. If they need a backrub, then give it with joy. If they need you to just hold them, then do that too. If they feel a need to make love, take a stroll on the beach or just sit and talk, just do it. It won't cost you anything, and will help them to feel your love.

Not only will they feel your love, but if they are being filled by God, just as you are, they are going to appreciate your love so much more. It will become something precious to them, like a prize that only they can win. Yet, a prize that they don't have to work to win, because it is given freely.

Action Items:

- Repent to God for not looking to Him to fulfill your need for love. Make a commitment to turn to Him, whenever you feel unloved or just a little lacking in love. Allow Him to fill your love tank to overflowing.
- Develop the habit of loving your spouse, out of the abundance of love that you have received from God, no matter whether they are loving you or not.

- Quit looking to your spouse to make you happy and instead learn to be filled with heavenly joy, regardless of your circumstances.

11

The Power of a Forgiving Heart

One of the biggest weapons that Satan uses against us is to create a bitter heart within us. Bitterness is a trap, binding us up and keeping us from doing the right things. More than anything, it keeps us from reacting to people as we should. Rather than reacting to them in love, we end up reacting to them out of the deep well of our bitterness.

Remember the familiar spirits I was talking about back in chapter four? Creating bitterness in our hearts is one of their main jobs. For when they can create that bitterness, they can destroy our testimony, as well as destroy any relationships that are affected by that bitterness.

But there's something else that bitterness does to us, which is essential to our current conversation. That is, it keeps us from dealing with ourselves. You see, bitterness comes out of offense, but more specifically out of blaming others for those offenses. We really can't be bitter towards others about something which we accept responsibility for. At the same time, we really can't accept responsibility for our own lives and attitudes, while we are busy being bitter towards others.

Let's face it, offenses come. Life is full of them. If anyone thinks they can get through a week without being offended by someone, let alone a year, they are living in a fantasy land. As long as there are imperfect people around us, there will be offenses to deal with.

And deal with them we must. Otherwise, those offenses will eventually end up dealing with us. Specifically, they will turn us into bitter people, who are constantly wallowing in our bitterness. That's a miserable way to live. I've seen people like that and I do not envy them.

To start with, we need to ask ourselves why we get offended in the first place. I mean, if offense is such an ugly thing, why would anyone want to have it? Wouldn't it be better to just opt out and say no thanks the next time it comes to call?

While that would be nice, it would require something of us that we don't really want to pay. For you see, when we get offended, it's because we feel like we have been given something negative, which we don't deserve. In other words, what the other person has said or done hits us right in our pride, which demands "justice." Since it can't have that ugly form of false justice, we become offended.

Did you catch the important word there? It's pride. We get offended because something crashes up against our pride and our pride pushes back.

But wait. Aren't we, as believers, supposed to get rid of pride? Isn't pride the original sin, the sin that caused Lucifer to fall and become Satan, and still one that our Father God loathes? How can we then, have so much of a problem with pride?

The fact of the matter is that many of us battle with pride. It's usually not the obvious sort of pride, which we are all quick to condemn, but the quiet, private sort. We don't allow ourselves to shout it from the rooftops, but we wink at that quiet sort of pride, just as long as we can keep it under control.

However, the very fact that we are offended shows that our

pride isn't under control, doesn't it? If it were under control, then it wouldn't matter to us what people said about us, said to us or did to us. Nor would it matter when people ignore us, forget us or act as if we are unimportant. All of this is a demonstration of how much pride we still have.

Could it be that God allows us to become offended, so that we can learn about the pride hidden in our hearts? Could this be another way in which God is using those around us to help us find our faults and come to a place of true godly change? I think it can.

If we honestly evaluate ourselves in the light of a Holy God, none of us deserves any of the good that He gives us. If anything, we deserve to be judged and found guilty of our sin. Yet God, in his infinite mercy and grace, has made atonement for us, in the form of his only begotten Son.

If anyone has a right to be offended, I'd say that God has a right to be offended by our actions. To start with, He is our creator. Then, He is our redeemer. Yet we, in our foolishness and pride, decide that we know better than God and do things our own way. We turn from Him, even as He is reaching out to us in love. What a tragedy.

But even in the midst of all that, God is not offended. He refuses to be. The one who has the most right to be offended is holding himself aloof from offense, not allowing it to touch Him. We see this manifested by His Son, Jesus, when He was on the cross. He said, *"Father forgive them, for they know not what they do"* (Luke 23:34).

Isn't that awesome? In a sense, we can say that He forgave us, before we even asked for forgiveness, simply because He asked His heavenly Father to forgive us. Obviously, Jesus didn't hold any bitterness in His heart, in spite of all that was done to Him, but rather chose to forgive.

That's the example for us. We too must learn how to forgive, without waiting for the other person to ask for that forgiveness. They may not even realize that they have offended us. So if we are waiting for them to ask forgiveness, we might find ourselves waiting an awfully long time.

Let me be clear here. Forgiving someone shouldn't have anything to do with them asking for forgiveness. Oh sure, if they come and ask for forgiveness we should forgive. But we shouldn't wait for that. We should forgive as soon as we realize that we are offended. The faster we can forgive, the better it is for us.

Remember, you aren't forgiving them for their sake; you're doing it for your own. You're the one who is bound up by the offense, not them. They're just fine, and your bitterness towards them isn't hurting them at all. I know that just doesn't sound fair, but that's the way it is. So holding something against them isn't accomplishing a thing, except to make you bitter.

This has got to be the one time when it's not only okay to be selfish, but it's highly recommended. I'll go even farther than that; being selfish about forgiveness is actually one of the most loving things you can do for your spouse. I say that because being selfish in this case, means being quick to forgive, so that you are not bound up by bitterness. You know something? In that case, both of you win.

Okay, so let's talk about the mechanism of forgiveness for a moment. Every once in a while, you'll hear somebody say, "I can't forgive, I still feel too much pain (or anger, or bitterness, or whatever).” But forgiveness isn’t a feeling; it’s a choice of your will. You choose to forgive and you speak it out of your mouth. Those words coming out of your mouth carry spiritual force to forgive.

By the way, you don’t need to tell them you are forgiving them. Getting in your spouse’s face and growling, “I forgive you, you louse” isn’t good communication skills, regardless of how tempted you might feel to do it. Unless they have asked for you to forgive them, your forgiveness is a private matter, between you and God. Take it to Him and leave it there.

This brings up another important point. How many times do you forgive someone, when they offend you? Is there actually a point you can reach, where you are justified in saying, “No more!” Let’s see what Jesus said about that.

> *Then Peter came to Jesus and asked, “Lord, how many times shall I forgive my brother when he sins against me? Up to seven times?” 22 Jesus answered, “I tell you, not seven times, but seventy times seven times.*
>
> *Mathew 18:21-22 NIV*

Okay, now here’s the question; how many offenses were there in those two verses?

Few people get this one right. Some try to multiply it out and get 490. Some try to come up with some other number, like 77. But the truth is, there is only one offense there. In the wording of both Peter’s question and Jesus’ answer, we don’t see any more than just that one offense.

The thing is, we can keep getting offended over and over by the same thing. This was another important lesson I learned, when I went through that year of emotional crisis. Those familiar spirits would take some action, word or mood of my wife and get me offended by it, over and over again.

So what do we do with that? As we've already discussed, the cure for offense is forgiveness. So, it's time to forgive. But here's what happens. We forgive the other person for whatever offense there is and for five minutes we feel better. Then those pesky spirits start their recording and we get offended all over again. Aargh!

Now what do we do? We've already forgiven, yet we're still offended. This is what Jesus was talking about in Matthew. Forgive them again; and if you need to, forgive them again and again and again and again and again. In fact, keep forgiving as many times as you need to.

How do you know when you've forgiven enough? It's simple, actually. When you get to the point where you can think of whatever it was that offended you, without it bothering you, you've finally made it. You're done forgiving. But as long as it bothers you, you need to deal with it again. Just forgive them again and get over it. How many times will you need to forgive? I don't know. There were days when I was learning this, that I had to forgive my wife 50 times or more, about the same stupid thing... but I did it.

Eventually my mind learned that it wasn't worthwhile to keep going back to the same things over and over and getting offended over and over again. It took a while, but I learned to forgive more quickly and more thoroughly. It wasn't easy, but it was much easier than being offended all the time.

I remember one specific example that really hit home. We were buying a house, and my wife started looking on Craig's List for furniture. Not finding much in our area, she ranged farther afield, looking at cities 200 to 300 miles away. I told her that was fine, but not to buy anything until we moved into the house, so that I wouldn't have to move it twice.

What do you think happened? If you guessed that she found and bought furniture before we were ready for it, you are right. So early one morning I hooked up a friend's trailer to my van and started driving, going to pick up the furniture. After hitting three cities and filling the trailer, I returned home something like three o'clock the next morning and unloaded the furniture into the house.

I had three hours to sleep, before I had to wake my wife up, and I took advantage of it. When I woke her at 6:00, she was all excited to see the furniture and ran around the house checking it out. Then she got ready and rushed off to work. She just forgot one little detail.

What was that detail? She forgot to say "thank you" to me. Now, let me say that there was no real requirement for her to say thank you, but it would have been nice if she had. It would have been especially nice because it would have blocked what the enemy did next. For next two weeks the familiar spirits had a perfect weapon to use against me. They hit me with it over and over again, till the point where I felt like my head should be bloody from all the blows it was taking. I was forgiving her, but the offense kept coming back up over and over again.

Finally, after two weeks, I told my wife the struggle I was having. I didn't blame her, but rather told her how the enemy was using her oversight to beat me down. That was all it took; she thanked me and the devil lost the weapon he had been using against me.

Forgiving your spouse is critical. It doesn't matter what they've done or even if they know what they've done. In fact, there's a pretty good chance that they don't know. Not because they are insensitive, but because it wasn't meant to be offensive. Go ahead and forgive them. The sooner you do the better.

This is so important, that our salvation literally rides on it. Right after Jesus taught His disciples what we know of as the Lord's Prayer, he said:

> *For if ye forgive men their trespasses, your heavenly Father will also forgive you:* 15 *But if ye forgive not men their trespasses, neither will your Father forgive your trespasses.*
>
> *Matthew 6:14-15*

Do you see that? If you and I don't forgive, we aren't forgiven by God. How can we possibly enter into heaven without being forgiven? Isn't that the base requirement? Isn't that what salvation is all about?

I can't afford to take a chance on that one, and neither can you. Jesus told us to forgive. That's enough. That carries the same weight as any other commandment He gave us. So... forgive; and do it quickly.

Action Items:

Make a list of everything your spouse has done to offend you and forgive them for it. You don't need to do it to their face or even tell them what you've been offended by, this is between you and God. Then, once you've forgiven them of everything on the list, burn it.

Do the same thing for every relationship you have, especially with those who are closest to you.

Develop the habit of instant forgiveness, whenever you feel offended. Keep on forgiving, until thinking about what they have done no longer bothers you.

12

Recognizing Your Own Faults

Perhaps the easiest thing in the world is to notice something wrong with someone else. We all seem to have this amazing radar, which quickly alerts us to whatever fault those around us might have. We don't even have to look hard, it just shows up on our radar screen and then from that point on, we are aware of it.

But the same can't be said of our own faults. That radar just doesn't seem to work that way. If we try pointing it at ourselves, all it does is show us how we are not as bad as someone else, always picking someone who is clearly worse at a particular character trait or skill than we are.

This doesn't, of course, mean that we don't have any faults. It just means that we have trouble seeing them. It's probably some sort of self-defense mechanism that we have built into us; but it's one that can cause a huge amount of problems. When all we see is our spouse's faults and can't see our own, we can easily convince ourselves that the whole problem with our marriage is them... we just married the wrong person.

This takes us into really dangerous ground, breeding discontent and starting us along the road towards harboring thoughts of divorce. Yet those are totally unfair thoughts. The Bible teaches us that none of us are perfect, so why do we have so much trouble accepting the idea that we could possibly be at fault?

There is none righteous, no, not one

Romans 3:10

For all have sinned, and come short of the glory of God

Romans 3:23

What if there was some sort of device which we could look into, which would reveal our faults to us? Would you be willing to use such a device? Are you brave enough to truly face yourself, with all your ugly parts exposed? Would you be willing to accept what that device says, without equivocation?

Well, such a device does exist. It's a bit hard to use and requires constant, regular application; but it will show you every fault you have, one at a time. This device is the Bible. One of its many wonderful attributes is that it is a mirror of our souls, showing us the innermost workings of ourselves, especially the parts that need some work done on them.

The Bible shows us all those places where we fall short of the fullness of what God has called us to be. In other words, it shows us where we have not yet attained to the stature of Christ, if we are willing to delve into its depths and pay attention to what it shows us.

You can rest assured that anything the Bible shows you about yourself is true. You can also be sure that each and every place where you fall short of God's glory ends up hurting your spouse in some way or other. Oh, it might not hurt them every day, but it will hurt them, over and over again.

The thing is that most of us tend to jump over those parts of the Bible which will show us our faults and focus on the parts which show us God's promises to us. But guess what? Changing us is one of the most important promises God has for us. He loves us so much, that He is unwilling to leave us the way we are. Instead, He wants to make us into the image of His Son.

> *For whom he did foreknow, he also predestined to be conformed to the image of His Son, that he might be firstborn among many brethren.*
>
> *Romans 8:29*

I know I've used that verse before in this book, but it's an important verse. God has been using it on me for the last ten years or more, as He has been teaching me the things in this book. So, I figure if it's good enough for me, then it's good enough for you as well.

Recognizing our own faults is really nothing more than accepting what God, His Word and the Holy Spirit say about us. It is a sign of true humility. It is also a sign that we are willing to do something about it. People who don't recognize their own faults expect others to change for them. People who accept their own faults are in a place where they can start dealing with those faults.

So, how do we truly hear those faults, so that we can understand what they are?

To start with, we need to pay attention to our own reaction to the Word of God, whether we are reading it or hearing it preached to us. What makes us uncomfortable? What causes our justifier mechanism to automatically kick into overdrive? What do we tend to try and ignore?

Anything that makes us uncomfortable, causes us to try to justify ourselves or that we try to ignore is probably something that we really need to hear. It's a sign that the Word of God is hitting a sensitive area in our lives, one that demonstrates that we aren't really as great as we like to think we are. Those are our faults, and they are the things that God wants to work on in our lives.

Another tool that we can use is to actually listen to the things that our spouse says about us. If there is something that they regularly complain about, it's probably something that we need to take a good close look at. This isn't a perfect tool to use, as some people will reflect their own failings onto their spouse, blaming them for it. Others may not say things that bother them, simply out of politeness. But by and large, the things that our spouses complain about are real and should be looked at.

But don't just try and look at it alone. Get some help; and not from your best friend either. This is the type of thing to take to your spiritual mentor and ask them about. If they are a true mentor, they will not only be able to tell you the truth, but will also be able to give you some insight into your spouse's thinking.

But it's not enough to just know and recognize our areas of fault; we need to do something about them as well. Keeping the same fault for years is a bit like keeping a dead cat, just because it used to catch mice. Maybe that fault served your old man in some way in the past, but it isn't serving you today. You're a new creation and you don't need whatever assistance you think that the fault gave you. You have God instead.

Speaking of God, you don't have to try and get rid of that fault on your own. God Himself, in the form of the Holy Spirit, is more than ready to help you get rid of that. It is one of the greatest works that the Holy Spirit does. He is the world's greatest heart surgeon, removing dead and rotting things from the heart, to replace them with fresh and beautiful things from God.

However, you do have to cooperate with the work that the Holy Spirit wants to accomplish in you. The Holy Spirit is gentle and will not beat you over the head to get you to His operating table. Rather, He will wait on you, until you are ready to make a change.

And change we must. If we are ever to be remade into the image of Jesus Christ, we must allow the Holy Spirit to help us destroy the old man, so that the new man may become predominant. That old man is destructive to ourselves, our spouses, our marriage and our family.

The first way that we cooperate with the Holy Spirit is to acknowledge that which He is trying to show us. In fact, we can do even better than that, asking for Him to show us our failings. He knows us better than anyone and is more than willing to show us where we need to change. He is also able to show us why we need to change, especially the benefit that the change will bring to our lives.

That benefit will motivate us to cooperate in the change process, as long as we keep it in the forefront of our minds. In that manner, we can use it as s filter for the experiences which we have, seeing them as spiritual and not just natural. We can literally see the changes that the Holy Spirit is working within us.

The second way that we cooperate with the Holy Spirit is to not fight against Him, when He is trying to do His work. Many times, that work makes us uncomfortable. As such, we have a tendency to avoid it. Yet, the longer we avoid it, holding on to the things we need to get rid of, the harder it will be on us, when we finally relent and allow the Holy Spirit to do His work.

Cooperating with the Holy Spirit means actively participating in whatever He is doing. Often, that means participating in any lessons that He is trying to teach us. To do that, we must recognize them as lessons, and seek for the spiritual meaning within them.

This is not easy. We are flesh and blood, living in a physical world. So we tend to see things on the physical/natural level. But those things are not the things we must see. We must have the veil before our eyes torn away, so that we can see through to the spiritual. Once again, the Holy Spirit will help with this, but only when we ask for Him to open our eyes.

We live in two realms at once, the natural and the spiritual. As our bodies and minds are dealing with this physical realm, our spirits are dealing with the spiritual realm. So, everything in life has a spiritual significance, no matter how big or how small. The challenge that faces us is to stop just looking at the physical and start looking at the spiritual.

Action Items:

- Start reading the Bible with the awareness of seeking out those things that bother you. Realize that those are the things that God wants to deal with you about.
- Review the things that your spouse complains about in you, asking the Holy Spirit to help you understand where you might be at fault.
- Ask the Holy Spirit to search your heart and show you where you are falling short of the glory of God. Make this a regular part of your prayer life; not every day, but at least once a month.

- If you don't have a spiritual mentor who will be honest with you about yourself, find one.

13

What Do You Expect?

One of the biggest traps we lay for ourselves and our spouses is the expectations that we have. We expect them to do, say and be certain things; after all, that's why we married them. If they don't live up to those expectations, even if there was never any agreement that they would, we end up feeling like we've been cheated in some way.

These expectations come from the root of what we want to receive, in our innermost being, out of our marriage. They may be reasonable or totally wacky, but to us, each and every one of them is both reasonable and important. Anything less just won't do.

We come by these expectations honestly. Some come from watching our parents or others who have successful marriages. Others come out of Hollywood. We might even have a few that we gained from the church, school or some professional associations. Still others are manufactured locally, during the time we were dating our spouse before marriage.

This last group is usually the biggest and the ones that are closest to our heart. Most of them didn't come out of the many long talks we had with our future spouse, but rather our own imaginations about what it would be like to be married to them. We all had some very real ideas about that, even if we never mentioned them to one another.

As long as we were dating, those were mere desires. They

were the stuff of dreams. As such, they weren't dangerous at all. Whether our future spouse would fulfill them or not lay off in a future we could not see, although we all thought we could.

But there's something that happens after marriage. Those things we had dreamed about while dating, move from being mere desires to becoming expectations. That's when the trap is set. Each and every expectation that we have is an emotional landmine, just waiting to go off. We don't realize they are, but they are. It's just hard to see that because of the stars in our eyes.

"So, what's wrong with an expectation?" you might ask. The thing is, we don't realize it, but each and every expectation we have for our marriage is also a minimum standard of behavior that we are imposing upon our spouse. We may never have articulated it and they may never have agreed to it, but the standard is there nevertheless, and we won't be happy with them unless they meet it.

This is easier to see, if I give you an example. Let's say that there's a man, and one of his expectations is that his wife keep the house clean. What that really means is that it had better be absolutely spotless; Windex the hot water heater in the basement clean. Nothing less will do.

Every day when that man comes home from work, he's going to be inspecting the house. Oh, it won't be a formal inspection and he probably won't even realize he's doing it. But because he has that expectation, he will be noticing whether the house is clean or not. He won't really notice what is clean, what he'll notice is what isn't. That will stand out like a sore thumb.

So he comes home one day and the whole house is spotless, except that there was a cockroach that just crawled out of the woodwork and died, as he was walking in the door. You can be sure that the one thing that he'll see isn't the clean house, it's that stupid cockroach. That's what he'll focus on, whether he wants to or not.

The next day, he comes home just like the day before and once again the house absolutely spotless. But this time, there is no intruding cockroach to attract his eye. So, he doesn't notice a thing. Everything is as he thinks it is supposed to be, so he doesn't say a word.

Here's the deal. Without consciously realizing it, he's grading his wife every time he walks in the door. But the grading scale he's using runs from minus 100 to 0. That's right, the highest possible score she can receive is a zero... and that's if everything is perfect. So, even if she does everything he wants her to, she gets nothing out of it. All she does is avoid receiving any negative points.

The problem is, most of us have more than one expectation of our spouse. In fact, we can have many. So, we've set up an obstacle course for them, that they have to negotiate every day. And the best they can expect to receive for successfully completing that obstacle course is absolutely nothing. They will get zero points. But at least they didn't get any negative ones.

I've got to say, women generally have more expectations of their husbands, than men do of their wives. I'm not really sure why things are that way; I just know they are. Perhaps it's because women are relationally oriented and start thinking of marriage as little girls, playing with their Barbie dolls. Their husband has got to be just like Ken, perfect in every way.

Of course, playing dolls isn't the only way that women gain an understanding of what to expect from the perfect male, Hollywood plays its part. Women and young girls are inundated with images of those perfect men, so that they come to expect that they really exist. Sadly, they are in short supply.

Those perfect men in the movies have a 20 person staff to make them perfect. They have writers, makeup artists, someone to take care of their wardrobe and a whole team of experts to take care of the honey-dos. When it's their wife's birthday, someone hands them a perfectly selected, perfectly wrapped gift. If he needs to give her flowers, someone hands those to him too. He doesn't have to think of any of that stuff, someone else does it for him. No wonder they're so good, they're nothing more than the front man for a well orchestrated organization, designed to make them look good.

While expectations can be a serious obstacle to having a loving marriage, I don't want to say that all expectations are wrong. Some are righteous. But even so, they cause the same sort of grading on the same sort of scale.

I do a fair amount of traveling, ministering in different places. At times, my wife is able to accompany me, but most of the time I end up having to travel by myself. When I am away, she has an expectation that I will remain faithful to her, no matter how far I travel or how long I'm gone.

That's a perfectly reasonable expectation for her to have. We could even say that it is a righteous expectation. Even so, it's an expectation. So it gets graded and scored like any other.

If I was to come back from a trip and she asked me "Were you faithful to me while you were gone?" (she doesn't do this) I would of course respond, "Yes." But that wouldn't gain me anything. She wouldn't give me a kiss, tell me that I was good or congratulate me on my fidelity. She might even have a headache that night, even though I've been waiting all week to be with her.

You see, all I've done is meet her expectation. I haven't done anything special. It doesn't matter if a Las Vegas chorus line invaded my hotel room and I jumped out the window to get away from them. All I did was meet her expectations. Nothing special... at least not in her eyes.

The big problem here is that expectations leave absolutely no opportunity for appreciation or reward. As I said, the best you can expect is to get zero points. That's not going to buy you anything.

But what if we could change that? What if we could take those things and put them on a scale where our spouse received positive points for doing things, even ordinary things, just because we appreciate that they've done them?

We can. All we have to do is to stop looking at those things as expectations and start looking at them as desires. A simple change in our attitude can create a huge difference in our reaction.

Don't get me wrong here. I'm not saying that we want that action from our spouse any less. Nor am I saying that we should totally give up on ever receiving it. All I'm saying is that we change how we view it in our own mind and heart. We move it out of the column of things that our spouse has to do, to even be considered acceptable by us, and move it into the column of things that when our spouse does, it makes us happy. Isn't that what a desire is?

So let's take that and go back to our example of the man who wants the clean house. One day, he decides to quit expecting that his wife keep the house spotless. Instead, he allows that particular thing to be a desire. The only difference between the two is his attitude.

Now when he comes home from work and sees a spotless house, he is pleased and compliments his wife. If that cockroach's cousin decides to do a repeat performance and die on their floor, he doesn't fix on that. It's still a dead cockroach and it mars the perfection of the clean home, but hey, the rest of the house is still clean. He's still happy, although maybe not quite as happy as the day he comes in and there is no cockroach performing dramatic interpretations on his floor.

What's happened is by moving the expectation to a desire; he has drastically changed his attitude towards it and towards his wife. In doing so, he has totally changed the grading scale he is using. Instead of being minus 100 to 0, it's now 0 to plus 100. The worst grade she can possibly get, if she totally blows it, is zero. But anything better than totally blowing it gets her points.

Do you see the difference that makes? It takes the image of our spouse in our mind, and transforms it from being negative to positive. No longer are we constantly upset that they aren't living up to our expectations. Now we're rejoicing in everything they do, even if it isn't perfect.

You can't have a positive attitude towards your spouse as long as you are constantly comparing them to a list of made up expectations. It's just not possible. Nobody, except the Lord Himself, is capable of living up to it perfectly, all the time.

By having those expectations, you are being unfair to your spouse and unfair to yourself. You're unfair to them, in that you've set a standard that can't be attained. You've denied them the opportunity to make you happy and receive the reward thereof. You're unfair to yourself, because you have set yourself up to be constantly disappointed. Through that, you are being unfair to your marriage, because you are not giving a place for appreciation and joy to flourish. The best you can expect is to have a few days where they didn't blow it so bad, that you can call the day "neutral."

Let me put a point on this chapter, before I end it. One of the areas where I had expectations of my wife was in our sexual life. God has given her and I a considerable amount of revelation about that part of marriage, which we've used to bless a large number of couples. But we've had our own struggles in that area.

As we've grown older, our health has suffered at times. This has meant that there have been times when we couldn't fulfill each other sexually. That bothered me enormously. Hey, I'm a guy, and even though I'm not a spring chicken (spring rooster?), I'm still interested. So when we couldn't join ourselves together in making love, it caused a lot of stress for me. By about the third day, I typically was getting pretty stressed out.

Why? Was it really because I had that much of a sexual need? No, it was because my expectation was not being met. So I changed. I stopped expecting sexual intimacy from my wife and started desiring it. What that did was that when times came where her health make it impossible for us to make love, I wasn't getting stressed out. I was able to take it calmly and patiently, waiting for her health to improve.

That's not to say that my desire diminished in the least; it didn't. I wasn't looking for some other means of release either.

No, what I was doing was putting our love life in the hands of the Lord, and praying for my wife to be healed. Then I was waiting for the answer to come.

If I can make this work in an area that is so important to men, I'm sure that you can make it work as well, for whatever expectations you have of your spouse. Change your attitude, and allow yourself to start enjoying what they do for you.

Action Items:

- Take some time to seek out those things that you have as expectations of your spouse. This may take some time, as some of them are so deeply ingrained in us, that we don't even recognize them.
- Make a conscious decision to turn those expectations into desires, so that your spouse has a real chance of doing something that you will see as positive.

14

QUITTING THE BLAME GAME

Anyone who has ever had children knows that kids are great at pointing the finger at each other when they've done wrong. But just because one child points the finger at the other, doesn't mean that the one pointing is innocent or that the other one did the crime. Children can pretty much be counted on to point the finger at someone else, no matter what. They don't want to accept responsibility for their actions.

I suppose they come by it naturally; after all, Adam did the same back in the Garden of Eden, when God asked him if he had eaten from the fruit. Let me paraphrase his response for you:

> *"Well, you see God, it's like this. It really wasn't my fault. That woman you gave me, she at the fruit first. Then she gave it to me. So it's her fault that I ate it. She was listening to the serpent and just went right along with what he said. Clearly, it's her fault. It's even the serpent's fault, but it's not mine. In fact, God, you made that woman over there, so it's your fault too. If you hadn't made her, she never would have given me that fruit to eat. So you see, I'm the innocent party here. You're at fault."*
>
> *Genesis 3:12 Paraphrased*

Okay, maybe I was laying it on a bit thick there, but you get the idea. That's the essence of what he said, it's just embellished a bit. The big point is that he didn't accept responsibility for his actions. How different would all of history have been, had he been willing to accept that responsibility and say, "Yes God, I sinned. Please forgive me."

We all do bad things and we all try to get out of receiving the blame for them. It really doesn't matter if there will be any punishment or price to pay for it. We still want to wipe our hands clean of the situation and pretend we had nothing to do with it. It doesn't matter if we're talking about a mass-murderer sitting on death row or a three year old child that spilled their milk, the reaction is the same. Prisons are filled with innocent men, just ask them; none of them have done the crimes they've been convicted of.

This goes on in marriage all the time too. Every marriage counselor in the world can tell you the script. A new couple comes in for counseling and it always goes the same. That first session is nothing more than a contest between the two, to see who can blame the other the most.

Generally speaking, the woman wins that game, simply because she talks more. But in reality, both marriage partners lose, because when we blame our spouse for something, we are blaming ourselves as well. Aren't we supposed to be "one flesh" (Gen 2:23)? If we are one flesh and one part of that flesh does something wrong, doesn't that mean that the whole of the flesh has done it?

In addition to that, we break something in the marriage; something that's hard to repair. That causes us to lose the respect, admiration and support of our spouse. Who can respect someone that verbally attacks them for their own failings, rather than taking personal responsibility for them? And what is this all for? Simply so that the person blaming the other can maintain their own self-righteousness in their own eyes? Is that truly worth all that much?

The Bible makes it clear that *"none are righteous"* (Rom 3:10). That's why we need the atoning work of the cross. So why would any believer even think that their own self-righteousness has any value? Why would they delude themselves into thinking that their opinion of themselves is more important than God's opinion of them?

Yet by focusing on maintaining their self-righteousness, they have made that decision, reducing the value of what God and His holy Word say about them. Essentially, they have stated that their opinion is more important than God's. Oh, maybe they didn't mean to do that, but they did it nevertheless.

The fact of the matter is, in any marriage relationship there is ample fault to pass around. Even more specifically, in any marriage disagreement, problem or fight, both parties are guilty to some extent. Perhaps one is should take it upon themselves to accept larger share of the fault than the other, but the "offended party" usually has some part in causing the problem as well.

Let me give you two classic, but controversial examples to show you what I mean, those of adultery and physical abuse. Before I do, let me state that I am unequivocally opposed to both adultery and physical abuse. There is no excuse for either. The adulterer or abuser must take full responsibility for their actions and deserves whatever condemnation they receive. But at the same time, the other marriage partner can exacerbate the situation.

This is actually very obvious in most cases of adultery, if one takes the time to dig into the couple's history. I say that because the adulterer is not receiving what they need out of the marriage relationship. Either their sexual or emotional needs are not being met, so the adulterer seeks fulfillment elsewhere.

Had the offended party put more effort into fulfilling their spouse's needs, rather than self-centeredly seeking just to have their own needs met, they might have been able to reduce or even eliminate the adulterer's desire to look elsewhere. So, while they are definitely the one who was sinned against, there is still a strong possibility that they are at least somewhat culpable for the crime.

Now, before anyone goes off the handle at what I just said, I fully realize that there are some people out there, even within the Body of Christ, who have an adulterous nature. Those people will commit adultery no matter what, even if their spouse tries to fulfill every need and fantasy they have. Those are obviously not the cases I am referring to. Regardless, even in those cases, the last thing spouse should do is give them an excuse to commit adultery. If anything, they should give them reason not to.

In the case of physical abuse, there are many abusers who only become physical when something triggers that abuse. It could be that their spouse is nagging them, has not done something that they should or even denied the abusing mate sexually. While the abusive nature is clearly in the individual's heart, it can be the offended spouse that is supplying the trigger. If they did not supply the trigger to cause the violence, they would not suffer it.

Once again, there are limits to how far this example can go. Some abusers are such, because of drinking too much. But then, we have to ask the question of why the individual drinks so much. Could it be that they do so because they are dissatisfied in the marriage relationship?

I have to say that there are plenty of exceptions in both of these cases that I am using as an example. I know a woman who was abused by her husband, no matter how hard she worked to live up to his expectations and make him happy. I also know of a case where a man was repeatedly in adulterous relationships, even after his wife forgave him and tried to do everything she could to satisfy him.

Once again, I do not condone these actions. People who commit sins of this magnitude have serious spiritual and emotional problems that need to be dealt with. For them to blame their spouses for the abuse they are piling on them is totally absurd. I am merely using them as illustrations of how the offended spouse could possibly be at least partially to blame for the situation.

Why do I say this? Because before we run off blaming our spouse for anything, no matter how grave the situation, we need to ask the Holy Spirit search our own hearts first; showing us what part we might play in their negative actions.

Being quick to blame, even in cases as extreme as these, merely ignores the problems in one's own heart. Each and every one of them should be a warning to ourselves to look for what we might be doing wrong, what wrong attitudes we might have, and what we could be doing better.

Don't forget that one of the reasons that your spouse is the way they are, is that God has chosen them for you, to be a tool in His hands, in His process of changing you. So, those things that you want to blame them for are probably are probably directly associated with some of the biggest things that you need to deal with in your own stinkin' heart.

If your spouse is chronically late, causing you a lot of stress, then you need to change yourself and become more patient. If they are too messy, you need to change your priorities and realize that they are more important as a person, than the neatness of your home is. If he or she is not as communicative as you want, you need to improve your own communication skills, so that you can draw them out.

Blaming and excuses are the number one reasons why we don't change and grow into the image of Jesus Christ. As long as we are blaming our spouse, we are not allowing God to work on us. Yet, as I've already mentioned, we have no capacity to change our spouse. The only one we can change is ourselves.

Yes, there are things our spouses do wrong. All of them do, even the most perfect. But you and I need to concentrate on ourselves and the baggage we're carrying around in our own hearts. That's the part which is our responsibility, not the supposed failings of our spouse.

Once again, there is plenty of fault to go around. We just need to find the part that belongs to us. Where are we falling short of our responsibilities towards our spouse? Where are we erring in our response to them? How can we improve ourselves, so as to elicit a better reaction from them? These are the questions that we need to ask... and to answer.

Be quick to take responsibility for your own fault and quick to admit it. I have said for years that the only winner in a marital dispute is the person who is first to say, "It's my fault. I'm sorry." All too often, we wait for the other person to do that, proving our own spiritual immaturity.

Yet if we can learn how to take responsibility for our own actions and attitudes, we can change the marriage dynamic. We become the adult in the room, who is willing to be responsible not only for ourselves, but for our marriages. Better yet, we give God the opportunity to work on us, transforming us into the image of His Son, Jesus Christ.

Dealing with ourselves is the best and in fact the only way we have of brining about any change in our spouse. As we grow and change, the way we interact with them will grow and change as well. One of the ways it will change is to reduce the amount of strife in the marriage. Even if that doesn't motivate them to change, it improves the quality of the relationship for both partners.

But there's also a good chance that it will show our spouse that they have need of changing as well. If things get to the point where we are showing ourselves to be more spiritually and emotionally mature than they are, they will eventually see it. It will pull at their ego, causing them to become more aware of their own need to change.

How and when that happens is totally beyond our control, as is the way that they ultimately change. That's between them and God. But it will have to be a change for the good, simply because any other sort of change will be self-defeating. It will show them to be even more immature, creating an even larger maturity gap for their ego to have to deal with. So, while they might momentarily go the wrong direction, there will be plenty of internal pressure for them to go the right one.

The truly mature person is one who accepts responsibility for their actions, especially their wrong actions. Isn't that one thing we judge the maturity of our children on? Had Adam been mature, that's what he would have done back there in the garden. Yet the vast majority of people never really mature fully. They reach a point that appears mature to themselves, and stop.

We could call this point of growth "spiritual adolescence." Just like in the natural, those who are spiritually adolescent think they mature. But to those who truly are mature, their lack of maturity is obvious. It comes out in a myriad of ways, most especially in wanting rights, without accepting responsibility.

This is most obvious in the children of our society when they reach the point of growth where they think they are old enough to engage in sex. In their minds, the ability to engage in sex demonstrates their maturity. But that is only biological maturity, physical maturity. True spiritual maturity is attaining the self-control to abstain from an immoral sexual relationship, even when it's handed to you on a silver platter.

Let us be the ones who become the adult in the room, by being quick to accept responsibility for our own actions. Once we do, let's allow the Holy Spirit to work within us, eliminating those faults and replacing them with something much better.

Action Items:

- Take some time to review the things that you are blaming your spouse for. Where are you at fault in those areas? If need be, ask the Holy Spirit to show you.
- Review the last month. In what ways have you not taken responsibility for your own actions and the consequences of those actions?
- Work on accepting responsibility for your actions, regardless of the consequences or how it makes you

15

Getting Rid of False Assumptions

In case you hadn't noticed, men and women don't speak the same language. Oh, we use the same words and we put them in the same order, but we're not saying the same thing. For a lot of words, men have one definition and women have another. By and large, the man's definition pretty much tracks with the dictionary, but the woman's tracks with her experiences related to that word.

This creates many problems in communications between the sexes. But those communications problems are nothing compared to the problems which are caused when we try to understand what the other person said, as if it were said by someone of our own gender.

Even so, we all do that. Men think that what women say is straightforward, just as if another man had said it. Yet women speak in nuances, inferences and innuendo, giving hints to what they want, rather than saying it directly. In fact, I'd go so far as to say that when a woman says she wants something, chances are really high that she really wants something else. Men miss the signals that women give all the time, because they are looking for a direct message.

This works in both directions, with women assuming that whatever a man says is filled with the same nuances, inferences and innuendo that she herself would use. In doing so, she reads all kinds of things into what the man had said, which aren't there. Sadly, he immediately becomes guilty of those things, at least in her mind, just as if he had said them. It doesn't matter if those insinuations were the furthest thing from his mind.

These differences in basic communication create a situation that is rife for misunderstanding, leading to lots of hurt feelings, anger, arguments and outright fights. In fact, I'd have to say that something like 90% of marital disagreements come about from these misunderstandings. Yet if the couple would take the time to ensure that they really understand what each other is saying, much of that would be avoided.

It is easy to blame these misunderstandings on your spouse, telling yourself that if they just thought "right" there wouldn't be any problem. But in reality, there is no such thing as thinking right. What is right for a man and what is right for a woman are two totally different things.

In reality, this is one of those places where there is more than enough fault to pass around. Both parties are equally guilty, either for not saying things clearly enough for their spouse to understand it or for not ensuring that the message they received was the message that was sent.

We should not be reacting quickly in any negative way to what our spouse says, but rather be using any anger, irritation or hurt as an indicator that there might have been a misunderstanding. If we accept at all the idea that our spouse loves us, why in the world would we think that they are intentionally trying to hurt or anger us?

About the only time that I've ever seen a married man or woman do or say something to intentionally hurt their partner was in the middle of a fight. At such a time, their anger can cause them to lash out in unpredictable ways, mostly in a misguided effort to protect themselves. Sadly, that usually means hurting the other in the process.

But that's not what I'm talking about. I'm talking about the misunderstandings that lead to those fights, not the ones that happen in the fights. I think it's safe to say that pretty much everything said or yelled in a fight is misstated. So, in those other cases we should be using the things that hurt or anger us as a warning; because it is in those cases that the likelihood that they are intentionally doing something to hurt or anger you are essentially non-existent. So why in the world do we assume that they are saying something just to get under our skin?

As we all know, we live in a fallen world. Rather than living directly under God the Father's rule and his rule only, the prince of this world is the Prince of Darkness himself, Satan. His kingdom is the opposite of God's, pretty much down to every little detail. One important way, at least for this discussion, is that his kingdom is negative, whereas the Kingdom of God is positive.

That's right; we live in a kingdom that focuses on the negative, even though we are not part of that kingdom. We are surrounded by negativity every day. The news we read, the way people talk and even the television shows we watch are all based upon negative things.

This is a bit like the old "glass half empty/glass half full" argument. Seeing it as half empty, is negative, whereas seeing it as half full is positive. Nevertheless, most see it as half empty and talk about is in that light. Likewise, they call a traffic light a "red light" even though it is green as much as it is red and talk about the chance of rain, rather than the chance of sunlight. Many of our everyday expressions focus on the negative, not the positive.

Living in such a society, it's no wonder that it affects us who profess Christ as well. Although we are citizens of a positive kingdom, the negative kingdom around us impacts how we see things and talk about just about everything. This happens in pretty much all parts of life, including marriage.

What this means is that instead of assuming a positive interpretation of what our spouse said, we assume a negative one, with all the ramifications that go along with a negative interpretation. In doing so, we assume that they don't love us, rather than that they do love us. We accept as a given that our spouses are bad people, who are out to do us harm, rather than who they really are, the person who fell in love with us and married us.

Granted, people change through the years, but it's rare that they change to the point where a good person turns into a bad one. So why do we assume that they do? Wouldn't it make a whole lot more sense to assume that they are good people and that the things they do and say are for our good?

There is nothing wrong with asking for clarification if you don't understand something your spouse has said. Actually, there's something very right about doing that. When we ask for clarification we are building bridges of communication, seeking ways to prevent misunderstandings from occurring.

If that is so, why don't we do so more often? Could it be that we are more interested in being individually right, than we are in what is right for our marriage? Are we so self-centered that we fail to see that our assumptions are hurting our marriage?

Or are we so full of pride that we can't even see the possibility existing that we have misinterpreted them?

Regardless of which of these is the real reason behind our failure to ask for clarification, our failure is demonstrating that we are much more carnally minded and much less spiritually minded than we think we are. We also demonstrate that our main motivating factor is not love, but something else. In other words, we have a ways to go to reach Christ-likeness.

Jesus would never make such an assumption about someone. Granted, He was God incarnate and had much more wisdom and understanding than any of us. But He is also the example, showing us the spiritual level we should all strive to attain. So if He wouldn't do it, we shouldn't either.

The same can be said for assuming that the way our spouses have been in the past, is the way that they will always be. Maybe you've had a long-standing issue with your spouse over some bad habit or character trait that they have. You don't even bother asking about some things, because you already know how they are going to react... or at least, you assume you do.

But what if they are changing too? If God is working on you to make you into the image of Christ, isn't God going to be doing the same thing to them? If that's the case, any assumption you make could be wrong. Even if they always did respond in a certain way, eventually they will change.

Failure to allow for your spouse to change is either an issue with pride or a lack of faith. It could be pride, in thinking that only you are changing and growing into the image of Christ. It could be lack of faith in not believing that God is working on them as well. Either way, it leaves you in a position of limiting your acceptance of what God is trying to do and is capable of doing. In that, you could become a stumbling block to your spouse's growth in Christ.

Rather than turning your magnifying glass on your spouse's habits and character, turn it on yourself. Where are you being part of the problem? How are you making the wrong assumptions? How could you be misinterpreting and misunderstanding them? What haven't you allowed the Holy Spirit to do in your heart, so that you will readily accept what God is doing in theirs?

Action Items:

- Develop a "check" in your brain, watching for things that you get angry or hurt about. Whenever those emotions crop up, verify that you really understood what your spouse was saying. Ask for clarification.

- Learn to throw off the world's manner of thinking negatively and start thinking according to God's Word and His ways. Those are positive. Part of this is assuming that what your spouse said was supposed to be positive, even if it didn't sound that way at first.

16

Focusing on the Good

I've got some great news for you. That is, that God the Father has given you an absolutely amazing, wonderful gift that he has given to nobody else... your spouse. Now, I know it might not seem that way to you, but it's the truth. King Solomon recognized this and so instructed his sons.

> *Whosoever findeth a wife findeth a good thing, and obtaineth favor of the Lord.*
>
> *Proverbs 18:22*

Now, before any of you ladies out there say that there isn't a corresponding verse referring to husbands, keep in mind that the book of Proverbs was written to men. Solomon was trying to pass his wisdom on to his son, which is plainly shown through his constant use of the phrase "my son" throughout the book. Since we widely accept that the Bible is gender neutral, we can apply the same rule here, and say:

> *Whosoever findeth a husband findeth a good thing, and obtaineth favor of the Lord.*
>
> *Proverbs 1l:22 paraphrased*

Does it actually say that? No. But if we apply the normal modern understanding of scripture being gender neutral, we have to accept that it is implied.

So, why am I belaboring this point? Simply because we tend to forget it over the years. When we get married, we are convinced that we have indeed been favored by the Lord, in giving to us the one and only perfect spouse in the world. But somewhere along the way, we lose that perspective and start complaining about them.

There are a number of reasons why this happens, some of which I've already discussed in this book. So I don't want to repeat them here. What I want to concentrate on in this chapter is turning the clock of our attitude back, and recapturing the awe we felt for our spouse in the early days of our marriage.

I remember a wonderful song a number of years ago, called "Touch of the Master's Hand." In it, an auctioneer was trying to sell an old violin, asking for a bid of a couple of dollars. But an old man came forward and took the violin, dusting it off, tightening up the strings and playing beautiful music on it. When the auctioneer received the violin back, he was no longer asking for a bid of a dollar or two, but asking for thousands. What was the difference? The touch of the master's hand.

We must remember that the Master, God Himself, has his hand upon our spouse. Maybe we don't see the good that He is doing in them, but that doesn't mean that it isn't there. It just means that we are blind to His amazing work. We need to ask Him to open our eyes, so that we might see.

The auctioneer's attitude about that violin changed the value he saw in it. Before he recognized the true value of it, he thought it was all but worthless. But once his eyes were opened, he realized what a treasure he had in his hands. His whole attitude and his actions were changed by seeing the true value of that old, dusty violin.

This is what happens to us in our marriages, except in reverse. We're the ones who let our spouses "collect dust" and lose their value in our eyes. How? By forgetting to see the beautiful person inside and what that beautiful person can do. We focus on the dust, not realizing that we are the ones who put the dust there.

That may seem like an unreasonable comparison to you; and you might even say that there's no way that you put the dust there. You might even go so far as to blame them for putting the dust there themselves. But you're wrong.

How did the violin get dusty in the first place? It did so because it had been set aside and ignored. If it had been being played every day, there is no way that it would have had dust on it. Not only that, but the strings would have been tight and the violin would have been ready to make beautiful music. The "old man" wouldn't have had to clean it off and tighten the strings; he could have just picked it up and played it.

So, when was the last time you "played" your spouse? I don't mean that in any negative way, like playing a trick on them or pretending to love them, when you secretly despise them. What I'm referring to here is doing the things that you used to do, which brought out the best in them? Maybe, just maybe, the reason you aren't seeing the wonderful things you used to see in your spouse, is that you aren't giving them any reason for those things to come out. Maybe you're not allowing them to come out.

Every relationship is give in take to some extent. Our spouse's actions towards us are often reactions to the things that we do, just as our actions towards them are often reactions to what they do. Who started that? You both did. Gradually, through the years, you stopped pushing the buttons that brought forth the good music and started pushing the buttons that brought forth the bad.

For many couples, this started after about a year of marriage, when the first baby came along. Up until that point, the wife's whole attention is focused on her husband and his is focused on her. As the day of birth approaches, that gradually changes, as the woman's nesting instinct kicks in and she starts preparing to bring the baby home from the hospital. But that doesn't diminish her attention towards her husband, as they usually prepare for that first baby together.

Then something happens... the baby arrives. Suddenly their lives are turned upside-down. Babies are very demanding (as I've already mentioned in this book) and the new mother finds herself struggling to keep up with her baby's needs. She becomes sleep deprived, having to wake up every two hours throughout the night to feed the baby. Her whole life ends up revolving around that baby and its needs.

Her husband ends up feeling the pinch in this. Men typically have trouble connecting with babies, even their own. No matter how much the daddy loves his child, he really struggles to relate to it until it is old enough to play with. But what he does notice is that his wife no longer has time or energy for him. The wonderful marriage they had enjoyed up to this point turns into something else. Something where he feels like an outsider, looking in on the relationship between his wife and child.

Now don't get me wrong here, I'm not pointing any fingers. I'm not blaming women and I'm not blaming babies. I'm just trying to explain what is going on emotionally. As with every other situation, there is plenty of blame to go around. In this case, what typically happens is that the man stops giving so much of himself to his wife, because he feels like he isn't getting anything from her.

That doesn't mean that the man is the villain in this story either. Some women have said that men should be more understanding. But that finger can be pointed in both directions; so let's not bother. Men can't understand what it is to be a woman, any more than women can understand what it is to be a man. Don't believe what the feminist movement has tried to say, telling us that there really isn't any difference between the two.

If we use the birth of that first child as a starting point, and it usually is, we can see a definite decline start to occur in most marriage relationships. We have to be extremely deliberate to prevent that, understanding what is happening and how it affects us. Even then, it can still happen.

But let us leave aside all the negatives that can come out of that event for one moment and focus on just one, how it affects our attitudes towards each other. I've just stated that once that baby comes along, the woman lacks time and energy for her husband, and that his reaction to that is often to stop paying as much attention to her. Hence, we have the beginning of the reaction and counter-reaction cycle that happens throughout our married lives.

There are other things that affect this throughout the years, but this is the beginning. Major life events can wreck havoc on any marriage, especially when we don't walk through them together, holding each other up. But to do that, we have to have a good relationship to start. So, the worse our relationship gets, the less we hold each other up and the more these life events can damage our marriages.

One of the worst ways in which this affects us is not so much in particular actions, but in the attitudes behind those actions. Just like the auctioneer in that song, we stop seeing the beautiful instrument that our spouse is and merely see them as someone we are going through life together with. Worse than that, we tend to see them as an impediment to our being able to live out our life as we want to.

Please realize that this is a natural result of not "playing" our spouse. We, each and every one of us, stop drawing the good out of them. We expect the bad and therefore see it, regardless of what they do.

So what's the difference between this and how a couple is when they get married? It's nothing more than perspective. At the beginning we all have a positive perspective, loving our spouse and seeing the good in them. But through time, that perspective is replaced by a negative one; one in which we see the bad and are blinded to the good. We even go so far as to reason away the good, calling it an aberration.

Okay, so how do we fix this? How do we stop seeing our spouse in a negative light and start seeing them in a positive light once again?

Nothing could be simpler. Quite literally, all we have to do is make a decision to do just that; to start looking for and seeing the good and to start ignoring the bad. It won't be automatic, but if we make a firm decision to do that and then put that decision to action, we will quickly start seeing the wonderful person that we fell in love with and married.

It's really that simple. We will see what we want to see. If we are convinced that our spouse is bad, then all we will see is the bad. But once we decide to look for the good, we'll see that. We'll find that person we once fell in love with.

It's not that the good wasn't there all this time; it's that we stopped focusing on it. They haven't changed. They're still the same person. Oh, they're older and have learned through their life experiences, but the basic person inside is the same, more mature, but the same.

The real beauty of this is that we can totally transform our marriage, simply by changing our own attitude. For you see, once we see the good in them, we'll start acting differently towards them. We will seek out those good buttons we used to push and start pushing them once again. We'll become the person they fell in love with, causing them to fall back in love with us once again.

Action Items:

- Make giving thanks for your spouse a normal part of your prayer life. Write a list of things about them that you are thankful for and make specific reference to those things in your prayers. Thank Him, as well, for the word that He is doing in their life.

- Ask your spouse to share with you the things that you used to do, to "play them," that you are no longer doing. Make a concerted effort to start doing those things again.

- What ways are you reacting negatively to your spouse? What can you do to stop that cycle and react in a positive way to them? I'm not talking about them changing something, so that you don't react negatively, but you changing something. Make those

17

LEARNING TO LOVE UNCONDITIONALLY

There's a huge amount of misunderstanding about love in the world and in the Body of Christ as well. What is often portrayed as love on the big screen is more correctly identified as lust or infatuation, yet that definition is the one that many people understand today. Unfortunately, we carry that misunderstanding into marriage, expecting the feelings we had during our dating and courtship to continue and even grow. When they don't we are disappointed and often disillusioned about marriage.

Yet we all continue to seek love more than anything else in life. The hunger to love and be loved causes us to enter into dating relationships, get married, have children and even at times enter into adulterous relationships. Basically, love, or more correctly, our misunderstanding of what love is, has the power to make a mess out of just about anything having to do with relating to other people, especially people of the opposite sex.

You may be thinking I'm all messed up here, "After all," you might say, "we get married for love; because we love the other person." Do we really? Is what we're feeling actually love or is it something else?

I think I can dispel that myth with one simple declaration about love. That is, love is other focused, not self focused. Based on that, can you really say that you got married because you loved your spouse? Or is it really that you loved how your spouse made you feel?

Ouch! That one hurt.

Yeah, it hurt me too. When my wife and I got married, I was sure that I had found the love of my life. I was also sure that I loved her more than anyone else could imagine. These two are not the same. You see, the first was true, in the sense that my wife and I are committed to each other. As part of that commitment, I have chosen to love her all my life. But it's the second one that's the problem; like everyone else, I loved what she did for me and how she made me feel. I didn't really love her, even though I thought I did.

Since then, I've had to learn what love really is, and I'm still learning. I think this is one of those lessons that goes on for our whole life. At least in my case it seems like it is turning out that way.

So how do we know what love is? That's easy, *"This is how we know what love is: Jesus Christ laid down his life for us. And we ought to lay down our lives for our brothers."* (1 John 3:16 NIV). The word there that is translated as "brothers" can mean either a literal or figurative brother in the Greek. So I would have to say that it applies to sisters as well as brothers. More to the point, since you're reading this book, which indicates that you're a Christian, it can mean either your husband or your wife.

So, when was the last time you laid down your life for your spouse? I don't mean literally accepting physical death to protect them, although that would definitely qualify as laying down your life, but I mean laying it down on a day-to-day basis, where you are willing to lay down your hopes, dreams and desires, so that they might have what they want. I also mean laying down your will, giving them your time, and putting them before you.

Guys, let me give you a perfect example of laying down your life for your wife. It's going to the mall, the day of the big game, and spending the entire day with her, clothes shopping. I don't mean trying to rush her though it, or trying to keep track of the game on your phone, I mean giving her your day, even though it hurts.

Ladies, how about making love with your husband, even when you don't feel loved yourself? I don't mean just allowing him to use your body; but rather being fully engaged in lovemaking, so that you can make him feel like you're the greatest lover that ever existed.

Aren't the things I listed a couple of paragraphs back all part of what the Bible teaches us we should be as children of God? Isn't that what it means to *"esteem others better than yourself"* (Phil 2:3)? For that matter, the examples I gave about laying down your life fall into that category as well. If we esteem our spouse before ourselves, shouldn't we be more concerned about them, than we are about ourselves?

I know this is a lot to swallow, but it's true. The love we have been deceiving ourselves with isn't a true love. It's a self-centered sort of love, where we are looking to receive from our spouses, rather than give to them. That sort of love breaks down into a non-verbal negotiation, like I talked about earlier.

Now here's what the Bible says about real love:

> *Love is patient, love is kind. It does not envy, it does not boast, it is not proud.* [5] *It is not rude, it is not self-seeking, it is not easily angered, it keeps no record of*

wrongs. [6] Love does not delight in evil but rejoices with the truth. [7] It always protects, always trusts, always hopes, always preserves. [8] Love never fails.

I Corinthians 13:4-8a

Yeah, I know, you've probably seen that passage of scripture so many times, that you just skipped over it and didn't bother to read it. But let me ask you something. Is there anything that you can find in those verses that is self-centered? I can't. All I see is that love is about doing the right thing for the other.

Is that the type of love you had for your spouse when you got married? I seriously doubt it. I'll freely admit that I didn't have it, although at the time I thought I did. But as I've already said, I'm still learning how to love her, *"as Christ loved the church"* (Eph 5:25).

The word that's translated as "love" in those verses is the Greek word *"agape."* We've all heard that word tossed around a time or two. It's that perfect, God kind of love that nobody really understands, but we all pretend that we do. Don't feel bad; the Greek's didn't understand it either. It was in their language, but until Jesus came along, they had never seen it in action.

Agape is actually a Greek translation of the Hebrew word *"haceed"* another word that escapes our understanding. Actually it escaped the understanding of the scholars who translated the Bible as well. At times they called it "love," but in other places in the Old Testament, they translated it as "mercy."

Haceed has its roots in the ancient custom of covenant, something that was practiced in Old Testament times, but had been lost by the time that the New Testament was written. That's why we have so much trouble with understanding it. Without true covenant commitment, we can't fully grasp haceed. But as I was studying it out several years ago, I felt that God gave me a definition of haceed. Allow me to share it with you:

> *Hacced is an overwhelming desire, to give of yourself, to the other person, for their benefit, no matter what it costs you.*

Let's take a moment to break that down.

- "an overwhelming desire" – it's an irresistible force, drawing you into an action
- "to give of yourself" – the only true gift you can give, which has any value, is something of yourself. Not something you've purchased, but something of you, the person. Whether that is time, energy, devotion, loyalty, strength or knowledge, it is still something that is an integral part of who you are.
- "to the other person" – it's centered on them, not on you. You can't have haceed if you are hoping to receive something in return.
- "for their benefit" – giving someone something that benefits you isn't a gift, it's a con job. You know, like a woman giving her husband tools for Christmas, so he'll do the honey-do list. That doesn't work, they have to be the one to derive benefit from it, and that has to be your focus.
- "no matter what it costs you" – this is the hard part. Love, true love, always costs you something. If it doesn't, I seriously doubt it is love. But the beauty of love is that it's a cost that you're happy to pay. In fact, you don't notice it as a cost, because of your overwhelming desire.

Now, based on that definition, can you really say that you've experienced agape/haceed love anytime in your life? Can you say that you have loved your spouse with that perfect a love? Ouch again.

Let me give you some good news now. You can learn to love your spouse with that perfect, unconditional love. Not only that, but you can reach a point of enjoying loving them that way, no matter what. How's that for a promise?

You and I were created to love. We know this, because we are created in God's image (Gen 1:26); and *"God is love"* (1 John 4:16). Love needs a recipient. In fact, it's driven to seek one out. That's at least part of why God created us, so that He could pour out His love upon us. But in making us in His image, he also made us creatures of love. One of our greatest desires is to love and be loved.

But God is perfect and so is His love. So, since we have been created in His image, that's the type of love we are created to give. Not the selfish love that seeks something in return, but a perfect, unselfish love that will blow your spouse's socks off.

How do we do that? First of all, we need to be filled with love, so that we have love to give. I talked about where we were supposed to get that earlier; from God the Father. Trying to express perfect love, based only on the love you have within you won't work. You don't have enough. You need God's love and you need it in abundance.

The next secret is this; love your spouse not for who they are and what they've done, but in spite of it. I know that goes totally against anything you've ever heard, but let me ask you something. Isn't that what God does with us? Doesn't He love us in spite of ourselves?

Loving your spouse in spite of themselves is actually much easier than it seems, if you're filled with God's love and have made a decision to love your spouse no matter what. It doesn't depend on your feelings; in fact, your feeling depend on it.

This is another of those lessons I learned the hard way, during that year of emotional crisis I went through. About halfway through the year, God started talking to me, telling me, "Today is a good day to buy your wife flowers." My less than gracious response was, "Lord, I'm having a bad day as it is, this isn't a good day to buy my wife flowers, it's a horrible day to do it."

Well… let me tell you a little secret here, just in case you haven't figured it out for yourself. Arguing with God is a waste of time. Every time God said that to me, whether it was flowers or a gift or cooking a special meal for her, I gave the same argument… and I lost.

Now, let me tell you the good news. This is big. That is, our emotions follow our actions. In other words, by obeying God and buying my wife flowers or a gift, I ended up feeling love towards her. Not only that, but all the bad feelings that I had before buying the gift seemed to go away. Showing unconditional love towards her, at a time when I felt that she least deserved it, ended up helping me. Isn't that crazy?

It didn't help me because of any way I twisted or manipulated the situation. Nor was it that I was buying that gift in order to get something out of it. It was as pure and unselfish an act as I know how to do. And I reaped the benefit from it.

You've probably heard people say that, "Love isn't a feeling, it's a decision." That's a bunch of hogwash. Love is a feeling, but it is also a decision. The feeling of love comes when we make the decision to act in love. That's the secret to giving your spouse more love than they have ever received before. It's also the secret to unconditional love. But even more than that, it's the secret to having the feeling of love towards your spouse, every single day of your life.

Action Items:

- Make a commitment to *haceed* your spouse, no matter how you feel or what they have done.
- Develop the habit of doing something special or buying something special for your spouse, the days that you feel the most unloved and mistreated.

18

Let Not the Sun Go Down...

Anger is destructive to the soul. It is like a caustic acid, destroying everything it touches. Giving enough time, it can even destroy life, leading us to kill those around us, whether figuratively or literally.

But many of us misunderstand anger. The first way in which we misunderstand it, is in misunderstanding what it is. Generally speaking, anger arises when we feel that we have been mistreated in some way or other. In other words, it comes out of pride. Yes, there are situations where we are angered by others being mistreated; but usually, we're angry because we feel we have been.

Of course, pride is the first of sins, the one which caused Lucifer to fall from grace and become Satan. So it's not surprising that he would do everything he could to implant it in us, God's highest creation. But we don't have to accept it. I've already discussed how we have the power to refuse anger any time we so decide.

But most of the time, we aren't honest enough with ourselves to call our anger what it is. Instead, we refer to it as an "irritation" or "annoyance." It can't be anger, because if it were, it might be an unrighteous anger and we can't have that.

Do you know what the difference between an irritation and anger is? It is nothing more than size. In fact, the only difference between the smallest irritation and a murderous rage is size. They are both the same emotion, one is just larger than the other. We essentially lie to ourselves in identifying anger differently, based upon how much of it we have.

Let's just call a spade a spade, or in this case, let's just call anger what it is... anger. With that decided, we need to decide how to deal with it. The Apostle Paul gives us some very clear instruction about that, in his letter to the Ephesians:

> *Be ye angry, and sin not: let not the sun go down upon your wrath: 27 Neither give place to the devil.*
>
> *Ephesians 4:26-27*

The first thing we find in those two verses is an admonition to not let our anger cause us to sin. This is important, because that is an extremely easy error to make. Many a person has sinned in their anger, later realized in horror what they did. So we need to watch over ourselves extra carefully when we find ourselves angry.

Please realize that I'm not just talking about what many would call "major sins" here. While some may commit adultery, rape and murder out of their anger, most of us would limit ourselves to verbally assaulting the one who made us angry, our spouse. Yet that is still sin. Don't try to tell yourself it's a "smaller sin," it's still sin. In God's eyes, they are both equal; and isn't His opinion the only one that really matters?

Let me jump over the middle part for a moment and go to the end. Verse 27 says, *"Neither give place to the devil."* This ties in directly with the first part, where our anger can cause us to sin. The devil loves it when we are angry, because anger destroys our reason. That makes it much easier for him to plant suggestions in our mind, often suggestions that we follow through on.

That's one of the biggest dangers of anger. It provides an open door to the devil, which he can then use to get into our lives and push us to do the wrong thing. Before we know it, we can end up doing everything we don't want to do and ignoring all the things we should be doing instead.

But I'd have to say that the key part of this verse is the middle part. That's where it gives us the instructions necessary to avoid the sin. Allow me to repeat it, *"Let not the sun go down on your wrath."*

This is where I gained the understanding that irritation, anger and wrath are all the same thing. Actually, it was my wife who got it from the Lord and shared it with me. The Lord had called her out on her wrath, and she responded "Lord, I don't have any wrath, I just have irritations" (Yes, I'm not the only one who has tried arguing with the Lord. But it didn't go any better for her, than it did for me). He responded, telling her that irritation was just a little wrath and wrath was just a big irritation. So, she had wrath. Ouch!

For years, I have understood this part of the verse to mean that we should resolve issues before the day ends. That way, there would be no reason for the anger to exist. But I was wrong. Like many others, I was reading things into the verse, which simply weren't there.

That phrase doesn't say *"let not the sun go down on your issues,"* it says, *"let not the sun go down on your wrath."* While the two may seem the same, they are not. Yes, we get angry over some issues, but we don't have to. In fact, we probably don't get angry over everything that's an issue between us and our spouses. There are some that are petty enough that we choose not to get angry over them, even though they are still issues.

I mentioned one of these earlier, when I was talking about my wife leaving bottles on the edge of our bathroom sink. While I don't get irritated over this and for years didn't even mention it, it was still an issue. What made it an issue was the fact that it inconvenienced me and that bothered me. But I made a decision that I wouldn't let it bother me enough to get irritated over it.

Actually, it was at the point when I first found myself getting irritated about it, that I made that decision. It was my choice, and I like to think that I made the right one. It wasn't important enough to even get irritated about.

Let me postulate something here. Anger and issues can be separated from each other. In fact, I believe that they should be separated from each other. When we do that, we are able to deal with the anger and get rid of it, even though the issue still exists. That's what the verse is talking about; getting rid of the anger, not getting rid of the issue. When we separate the two from each other, it actually becomes possible to do just that.

In that case, we can eliminate the anger before the sun goes down, leaving the issue to be dealt with at another time. How do we do that? By forgiving them for the thing that has made us angry in the first place. Remember, forgiveness does not require that the other person ask for forgiveness or that we discuss why we are in anger. It doesn't even require that we talk to them. Forgiveness is between us and God; nobody else.

Holding on to the anger, just because the issue has not been resolved, is both foolish and dangerous. When we do that, we are setting ourselves up for failure in one way or another. Personally, I'd rather avoid that failure and get the forgiveness out of the way.

One we have forgiven, it is easy to schedule a time to discuss the issue. Better yet, the issue will actually be discussed, rather than fought about. Isn't that great? By separating the two, we give ourselves the chance to actually come into agreement about a solution, without having the extra baggage that is caused when we start fighting and hurt one another.

That doesn't have to be done before the sun goes down or even in the same day; but you shouldn't wait too long. The longer you wait, the more of a chance there is for the issue to come up again. So make sure to schedule the issue resolution discussion fairly quickly, in a couple of days at the most.

Let me take this idea a step further. If we can separate the issue from the anger in order to follow the instruction given to us in that verse, then we can do so any time we have a disagreement as a couple. Rather than allowing ourselves to get into a fight about it, we can instead choose to stop for a little while, so that both parties can take a moment to forgive and get rid of their anger. Then, when that is done, we can come back together to discuss the thing that made us angry in the first place.

In other words, I'm talking about agreeing together to not deal with things when you are angry, but rather to deal with the anger and the issues separately. If you do so, then you will find it much easier to solve the problems you have between each other.

If our goal is to resolve the issue, rather than just to demonstrate our negative emotions, regardless of how much hurt they cause, then this makes a whole lot more sense. It's always easier to come to a reasonable solution when both parties are thinking clearly and not overrun with negative emotions. What previously would have been cause for a fight could instead become the opportunity for a construction discussion and a healthy solution that meets both of your needs.

Action Items:

- Make a decision to start separating your anger from the issues which you are allowing to cause it. Then get rid of the anger by forgiving your spouse. If you find yourself getting irritated about it again, forgive them again. Do that as many times as you need to.
- This is one chapter that I would highly recommend discussing with your spouse, coming to an agreement that you will separate your anger from your issues and each deal with the anger separately. That way, you will be able to better deal with the issues.

19

So Where Do You Go From Here?

By now you might be feeling a bit overwhelmed by what I have given you in this book. If not, might I politely suggest that you read it again and pay attention to what you're reading this time? I can tell you this, there were many times I felt overwhelmed as I was learning it. These are not easy lessons to receive, at least, not if you take it seriously.

But if you're like many believers, you're probably going to make excuses about why you can't make the changes that I've talked about here. The most common of these excuses will be:

- If God wants it, He'll have to do it
- If my spouse changes first, then I'll change
- If this is what God wants, he needs to give me a sign
- But my spouse is the problem
- They don't deserve me treating them that well

Let's just call all of those excuses what they are... garbage, and throw them out where they belong. None of us are ever going to reach the fullness of what God intends for us, as long as we are making excuses. We've got to take responsibility for who we are, what we are doing and what we are failing to do. Then and only then, do we stand a chance of being the people that God has created us to be.

God's plans and aspirations for our lives are so much higher than our own. He doesn't see us as we are, but rather as he wants us to be. That's seeing us through the eyes of faith.

The thing is, believers complain all the time about not seeing God's blessings in their lives. Well, let me tell you a little secret. Those blessings don't come from twisting God's arm with our faith; they come when we are obedient children who are growing into the people that He wants us to be. In other words, if you want God's blessing, you've got to obey Him first.

The things that I've talked about in this book will transform your marriage. But it won't stop there. The very same attributes that you're going to be working on for your marriage, are also going to affect other areas of your life. You'll find blessings in your work, in your family, in your church and in your other relationships as well. It's just that your marriage is going to be the tool which the Holy Spirit will use to show you what needs to change.

Don't try to do everything I've talked about in this book, all at the same time. Just as I told you to read it a chapter at a time, work on the different areas that you need to improve on one at a time as well. There's no way that you can do it all at once, so take the time to do one area right. Then, when you've got that area working pretty well, it's time to move on to another one.

You can always come back to an area, if you see a need later on. In fact, I'd almost bet that you'll have that happen. That's okay. It just means that you've grown as much in that one area as you can for the time being. After working on something else, it will be easier to go on.

Above all, don't give up on yourself. Yes, you will fail; we all do. But the difference between a failure and a success is that the success gets up one more time than they fall down. So when you fall, forgive yourself, ask your spouse to forgive you and get back in the game again.

If you want some real accountability on this journey, tell your spouse what you are doing. They'll let you know how well it's working out. Or, better yet, take this journey together, holding each other's hand and helping each other along. Working on it together will help draw you together and bond together as one.

God's desire is for you to have a blessed, joyful, even sexy marriage. As you fulfill these various stages in your growth, you should see that begin to come about. If not, check yourself and see where you are falling short. Once again, it will show you something that you need to change in your heart, so that you can go forward in life and marriage.

God Bless You!